Contributions to Finance and Accounting

The book series 'Contributions to Finance and Accounting' features the latest research from research areas like financial management, investment, capital markets, financial institutions, FinTech and financial innovation, accounting methods and standards, reporting, and corporate governance, among others. Books published in this series are primarily monographs and edited volumes that present new research results, both theoretical and empirical, on a clearly defined topic. All books are published in print and digital formats and disseminated globally.

Milan Bednář

Fiscal Policy in the Southern European Union Countries

The Aftermath of COVID-19

Springer

Milan Bednář
Department of Economic and Social Policy
Prague University of Economics and
Business
Prague, Czech Republic

This book was prepared with the financial support of the Internal Grant Agency of the University of Economics in Prague, grant number: IGS F5/27/2021.

ISSN 2730-6038 ISSN 2730-6046 (electronic)
Contributions to Finance and Accounting
ISBN 978-3-031-29760-1 ISBN 978-3-031-29761-8 (eBook)
https://doi.org/10.1007/978-3-031-29761-8

This Springer imprint is published by the registered company Springer Nature Switzerland AG
The registered company address is: Gewerbestrasse 11, 6330 Cham, Switzerland

Review Summaries

The monograph provides an insightful and comprehensive analysis of the fiscal situations of some of the most indebted countries in the world. The author uses a rigorous analytical framework and a wealth of data to offer a detailed and comprehensive analysis of the fiscal situations of the EU4 countries. The book's comprehensive analysis, rigorous methodology, and policy recommendations make it an essential reading for anyone interested in understanding the fiscal challenges facing the EU4 countries and the possible policy measures that can be taken to address them.

prof. Ing. Erika Pastoráková, Ph.D., Dean of the Faculty of National Economy, University of Economics in Bratislava (Slovakia)

The monograph contains valuable new insights regarding both qualitative and quantitative analyses. For instance, I appreciate the estimations of structural budget balances, fiscal multipliers, fiscal determinants, and fiscal projections, including sensitivity analyses. This book is addressed primarily to researchers and policymakers. However, its value added will contribute to a broader audience, including doctoral students or public officers involved in the area of public finance.

doc. Ing. Eva Zamrazilová, CSc., Deputy Governor of the Czech National Bank (Czech Republic)

Acknowledgements

I sincerely thank my colleagues at the Department of Economic and Social Policy of the Faculty of Economics, Prague University of Economics and Business in Prague, Czech Republic, for creating an inspiring environment that has led to this book.

Furthermore, I would like to thank my family and friends for many years of support, without which this book would not exist.

About This Book

In 2020, European countries were hit by an unprecedented shock, which produced striking political and macroeconomic reactions and ultimately led to another round of significant public debt hoarding within the European Union (EU) and the Euro Area. This fact represents one of the most complicated challenges regarding modern fiscal policy-making. At this moment, European leaders are once again trying to find a solution to the unsustainable development in the EU, particularly in the Euro Area. Nevertheless, the dire situation of many EU countries has its roots in previous developments. At the same time, we live in the era of (dis)information, wars, and improper analyses, which makes the situation even more difficult.

Therefore, this book offers a positive and in-depth analysis of the fiscal situations of some of the most indebted countries in the world. These are the EU4 countries of Italy, Spain, Portugal, and Greece. At first, the book discusses the role of fiscal policy in developed economies. It describes key mechanisms of debt transmission, discusses the potential establishment of fiscal and debt union in the EU, identifies numerous implications, and connects the fiscal positions of the EU4 countries with other factors, namely with the structural flaws of the Euro Area and the common monetary policy of the European Central Bank. Later, all these aspects are considered and used for a detailed analysis of the fiscal situations and policies of the EU4 countries. The work analyses the macroeconomic standing of the EU4 countries, provides relevant macroeconomic and fiscal benchmarks, and presents an estimation of structural budget balances, including a detailed discussion and comparison with the estimates of major international institutions such as the IMF, OECD, and European Commission.

Furthermore, it identifies key drivers of debt dynamics in the EU4 countries and provides relevant projections of government debts. A separate chapter is devoted to analysing the fiscal policy determinants of the EU4 countries, using time series since the late nineteenth century, and the issue of fiscal policy efficiency. Finally, the work provides an overview of possible debt resolution options and proposes relevant economic policy measures. Overall, this book offers eight core chapters intended for the public, professional economists, and policymakers simultaneously.

Contents

About the Author

Milan Bednář is a graduate of the Prague University of Economics and Business, Czech Republic, where he obtained his PhD in Economic Policy. Formerly, he also studied at the University of Queensland, Australia, and cooperated with selected universities, such as Shanghai University. Currently, he is an Assistant Professor at the Department of Economic and Social Policy at the Faculty of Economics of the Prague University of Economics and Business, Czech Republic. He is a lecturer of various courses, including European Union and Its Policies, Introduction to Economic and Social Policy, Monetary Policy and Business Cycle, Macroeconomic Analysis, and Applied Econometrics. His research focuses on macroeconomic analysis of European countries and policy-making in the European Union.

Abbreviations

AR component	Autoregressive component
BVAR model	Bayesian vector autoregressive model
CPI	Consumer price index
EC	European Commission
EC model	Error correction model
ECB	European Central Bank
EDP	Excessive Deficit Procedure
ELB	Effective Lower Bound
ESA	European System of National and Regional Accounts
EU	European Union
EU4	Examined countries: Italy, Spain, Portugal, and Greece
EU19	19 countries of the Euro Area
EU27	All the 27 countries of the European Union (as of 2022)
EMU	Euro Area, European Economic and Monetary Union
EUR	Euro currency
FC	Financial crisis of 2008–2009
GDP	Gross domestic product
GNI	Gross national income
HAC errors	Heteroskedasticity- and autocorrelation-consistent errors
HICP	Harmonised index consumer prices
HP filter	Hodrick-Prescott filter
IMF	International Monetary Fund
IRF	Impulse-response function
MIP	Macroeconomic Imbalance Procedure
N/A	Not available
NAIRU	Non-accelerating inflation rate of unemployment
NEER	Nominal effective exchange rate
OCA	Optimum currency area
OECD	Organisation for Economic Co-operation and Development
OLS	Ordinary least squares

PPP	Purchasing power parity (or parities)
PPS	Purchasing power standard (or standards)
PPT(S)	Percentage point(s)
REER	Real effective exchange rate
SNA	System of National Accounts
UC model	Unobserved components model
USA	United States of America
VAR model	Vector autoregressive model
YoY growth	Year-over-year growth
ZLB	Zero Lower Bound

List of Figures

List of Tables

Chapter 1
Introduction

In 2020, the coronavirus crisis hit many European countries. It was an unprecedented shock that produced striking political and macroeconomic reactions, ultimately leading to another round of significant public debt hoarding within the European Union (EU) and the Euro Area. Unfortunately, the shock was later complemented by the Russian invasion of Ukraine and the associated energy crisis. Nevertheless, the dire situation of many EU countries has its roots in previous developments. The financial crisis, which manifested between 2008 and 2009, uncovered significant economic issues in the Euro Area as it hit many economies and transformed into the European sovereign debt crisis. Moreover, we live in an era of (dis)information, wars, and improper analyses, which makes the situation even more difficult. For instance, many individuals thought the European debt crisis was no longer present due to the resurgence of economic growth after 2014—in the pre-COVID era. These statements were misleading because the recession ended, but not the systemic economic and debt crisis. At this moment, European leaders are once again trying to find a solution to the unsustainable development in the EU, particularly in the Euro Area. The occurrence needs to be analysed appropriately, and many aspects must be considered.

Currently, some of the Southern EU countries show extremely high levels of indebtedness and are now among the most indebted countries in the world. This fact represents one of the most complicated challenges regarding modern fiscal policy-making. Policymakers often claim that basic macroeconomic policies (including fiscal policy) can solve many economic issues, including structural flaws. However, many of these statements can result from the political process or unintentional ignorance. Politicians, who are short-term oriented or lack accurate information, continuously try to improve the situation by introducing various regulatory and stimulus packages. The regulatory packages, including the Stability and Growth Pact, the Fiscal Stability Treaty, or various monitoring procedures, such as the Macroeconomic Imbalance Procedure, result from political compromises and are presumably not very useful.

M. Bednář, *Fiscal Policy in the Southern European Union Countries*, Contributions to Finance and Accounting, https://doi.org/10.1007/978-3-031-29761-8_1

Furthermore, the role of the common monetary policy of the European Central Bank (ECB) is equally important. The policy has been expansive and based on prohibitively low interest rates since its beginnings. The fact was reinforced by the introduction of quantitative easing programmes by the ECB in 2010. The problematics require a positive economic analysis based on sound theoretical and empirical evidence.

The topic is relatively broad and has been discussed in a large number of books, studies, and analyses. However, I could not find a comprehensive work that would evaluate the issue from all major economic perspectives while focusing on a detailed quantitative analysis of the standings of the Southern EU countries. It should be noted that sole fiscal analysis is not sufficient due to the broad nature of the topic. To the best of my knowledge, the relevant literature lacks a coherent and sufficiently comprehensive analysis that combines an overview and evaluation of possible solutions to the problem of unsustainable fiscal policies in the Euro Area. Furthermore, few studies attempted to summarise all the relevant debt mechanisms and implications in the monetary union. Finally, the literature lacks comprehensive quantitative research, which uses identical methodology and is comparable among the Southern EU countries.

The present work offers a positive and in-depth analysis of the fiscal situations of some of the most indebted countries in the world. These are the EU4 countries of Italy, Spain, Portugal, and Greece. Moreover, it analyses the period of 2000–2021 for three reasons. First, it is a period that represents the beginnings and the current development in the Euro Area, including the effects of COVID-19. Second, the time frame is sufficiently long while it is still manageable to provide a detailed analysis of the issues. Third, the availability of macroeconomic data is considerably better after 1999. The work primarily focuses on macroeconomic aspects due to the broad nature of the examined topic. For example, it does not examine the detailed structure of government budgets, but it focuses on the relevant budgetary aggregates in the form of revenue and expenditure. Moreover, it strictly distinguishes between short- and long-term macroeconomic effects.

In this book, the reader will find a positive economic analysis and discussions regarding the role of the fiscal policy in developed countries, the interaction between fiscal and monetary policy, the Euro Area's institutional characteristics and its flaws, sovereign debt channels and relevant mechanism in the Euro Area, including the potential establishment of a fiscal and debt union in the EU. Moreover, the work stresses the impact of the common monetary policy of the ECB and its implications for the fiscal policies in the Euro Area. Subsequently, all these aspects are considered and are used for a detailed qualitative and quantitative analysis of the fiscal situations and policies of the EU4 countries.

This work analyses the macroeconomic standing of the EU4 countries in the EU and the world. It provides relevant macroeconomic and fiscal benchmarks. Moreover, it presents an estimation of structural budget balances, including a detailed discussion and comparison with the estimates of major international institutions such as the IMF, OECD, and European Commission. Additionally, key drivers of debt dynamics in the EU4 countries are identified, along with providing projections of government debt of the respective countries. A separate chapter is devoted to analysing the fiscal policy determinants of the EU4 countries, using data since the late nineteenth century.

Further, the work includes estimates of fiscal multipliers or fiscal policy efficiency in the EU4 countries. Finally, the work aims to provide an overview of possible debt resolution options and propose relevant economic policy measures. Throughout the text, the focus is on examining the key fiscal and debt mechanisms to understand what is currently happening in the Euro Area and the EU4 countries.

This book offers eight core chapters dealing with the examined topic coherently and logically. Hence, it is intended to read the text in the given order. However, the individual chapters can be read separately, as relevant interconnections with the other chapters are mentioned throughout the text. I hope that the readers will find this book useful because it is intended for the public, professional economists, and policymakers at the same time. For this reason, the book contains separate boxes that address technical details regarding various statistical estimations and calculations. These aspects are not vital for understanding the presented text.

Chapter 2
Fiscal Policy and Government Debt in the Twenty-First Century

The second chapter focuses on the definitions and the implications of the most fundamental concepts related to various fiscal analyses used in the other parts of this work. However, many of the issues are very complex and can fill a whole book. Therefore, the text provides only a brief overview that deals with the most crucial aspects regarding the topic of this work. The presented concepts serve as a baseline for a detailed description of other, more sophisticated notions used in the following chapters. In addition, the theoretical knowledge presented in this chapter is essential for a proper understanding of the issues and implications of the presented analyses.

This chapter is structured into five sections. First, it defines the basic principles of fiscal policy. Then, it follows with basic definitions of government debt and related concepts, which are used throughout this work. Subsequently, it identifies the interaction between fiscal and monetary policy and focuses on the influence of monetary policy over the fiscal setting. In addition, it briefly summarises the adverse effects associated with excessive debt accumulation. Finally, it discusses various approaches to sovereign debt sustainability assessments.

2.1 Basic Principles of Fiscal Policy

The concepts presented in this section are well-known and, for example, Barwell (2016), Cottarelli et al. (2014), and Langdana (2016) provide an up-to-date overview of the issues. The section provides only a summary of the main aspects.

Fiscal policy is one of the key macroeconomic stabilisation policies (sometimes called demand-driven or short-term economic policy).[1] Fiscal policy can be defined

[1]However, the adjectives in the brackets are not precise. Fiscal policy is able to influence both economic supply and long-term outcomes. Therefore, it is necessary to refer to specific concepts such as fiscal sustainability.

M. Bednář, *Fiscal Policy in the Southern European Union Countries*, Contributions to Finance and Accounting, https://doi.org/10.1007/978-3-031-29761-8_2

as a systematic effort of a government[2] to influence the country's economy. For this purpose, the government uses budget revenues (primarily tax collection) and expenditures (secondary redistribution) in the broadest sense. In addition, it is appropriate to separate terms that are sometimes incorrectly used as synonyms, i.e., budget policy and budgetary policy. The former focuses on the financial aspects of the realisation of government objectives. It is a narrower view, considered less macroeconomic and more microeconomic-oriented. The latter refers to budget balances, which should be either balanced or in a surplus. This work focuses on fiscal policy, which is a strictly macroeconomic view.

The basic functions of fiscal policy include redistribution, resource allocation, and macroeconomic stabilisation (for example, see Cangiano & Mottu, 1998). A regulation function could also be mentioned separately. However, it is an umbrella term because it includes the other main functions. The redistribution is essential for the implementation of social policies, prevention of poverty, and maintenance of social peace. The allocation function aims to improve efficiency in the given economy.

Nevertheless, it is often abandoned at the expense of inefficient redistributive policies that serve the interests of politicians and maintain social peace. Finally, the stabilisation function often refers to the Keynesian approach[3] to the aggregate demand stimulation economic policy. The concept may seem appealing in economic theory but is intrinsically problematic in policy-making practice.

The main objective of fiscal policy consists of the traditional macroeconomic objectives, including economic growth, price stability, and low unemployment. It is essential to distinguish between policy stances: expansionary, restrictive, and neutral. However, the practical determination of these stances, which are based on systematic government efforts, is complicated in practice.[4] The analysis of fiscal policy needs to be conducted using both flow (e.g., budget balances) and stock (e.g., accumulated debt) indicators. Keynesian economists argue that expansionary fiscal policy should be used during recessions to smooth the business cycle[5] (decrease its volatility). The expansionary fiscal policy boosts economic growth through increased government spending or lower tax rates.

---

[2]I neglect the political dimension and use the term '*government*' solely. Some countries, however, are characterised by presidential systems.

[3]The term is connected to a theoretical economic framework inspired by the work of John Maynard Keynes (1883–1946).

[4]The issues are discussed in the seventh chapter in the context of the presented analyses.

[5]The business cycle is the downward and upward movement of gross domestic product (GDP) around its long-term growth trend (potential GDP). It usually lasts between 4 and 8 years. However, its length is changing over time and is country specific. Currently, it is longer than in the past due to expansionary economic policies.

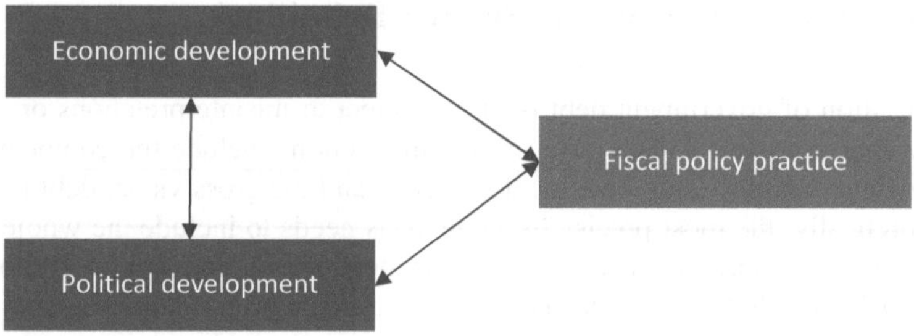

Fig. 2.1 Relationship between fiscal policy-making and real economy. Source: Own processing

Nevertheless, the recommendation, combined with the political process,[6] led to prolonged government deficits and debt accumulation in the modern advanced democratic economies (for instance, see IMF, 2022). Moreover, the analysis is complicated due to complex interconnections between fiscal policy practice and the real economy. The issue is simplified and illustrated in Fig. 2.1.

As it was mentioned, the practice of fiscal policy is problematic. First, a government may be subject to information asymmetries, including a lack of precise data or inappropriate assessment of the current state of the economy. The latter can be considered as the so-called government failure.[7] The failures result from various issues, including, inter alia, principal–agent coordination problems, regulatory capture, and corruption. Second, fiscal policy practice suffers from data lags, including data, recognition, legislative, implementation, and effectiveness lag. Third, the literature often emphasises the pro-cyclical nature[8] of fiscal policy, which is problematic[9] (refer to Barhoumi et al., 2018). Finally, the current monetary policy in the EU employs quantitative easing programmes, which significantly influence the redistribution processes and interact with fiscal policies. The issue is discussed in Sect. 3.3 in greater detail.

[6]The political process can be defined as all the circumstances connected with the processes taking place in the political markets where voters elect politicians while politicians seek funding for their election campaigns and fulfil their individual goals.

[7]As opposed to market failure, which is often identified as the problem. However, this is often not the case.

[8]It can be defined as fiscal stimulation during economic expansion.

[9]Fiscal policy aimed at macroeconomic stabilisation should be anti-cyclical by definition.

2.2 Government Debt and Related Definitions

The definition of government debt is often subject to misinterpretations or specific country characteristics.[10] The most critical distinctions include the composition of the relevant economic (sub-)sectors, debt items, and the gross vs net debt issue.

Theoretically, the most precise fiscal analysis needs to include the whole public sector, which comprises the general government sector and public corporations (refer to Bloch & Fall, 2015). Nevertheless, fiscal data are usually only analysed at the general government level. The data about the whole public sector are scarce and historical values are often unavailable (see Eurostat, 2022). Hence, this work uses data from the general government sector primarily. According to Eurostat (2013, p. 44), the general government sector consists of '*institutional units which are non-market producers whose output is intended for individual and collective consumption, and are financed by compulsory payments made by units belonging to other sectors, and institutional units principally engaged in the redistribution of national income and wealth*'. It incorporates four subsectors: central government, state government, local government, and social security funds. However, it is dependent on the individual country.[11] Besides, general government debt is usually different from 'state' debt. The latter is thus a narrower definition related to the state budget (Vebrová & Rybáček, 2014).

According to Eurostat (2016), the relevant general government debt within the Excessive Deficit Procedure (EDP)[12] is defined as the total consolidated gross debt at face value. It consists of the following government liabilities: currency and deposits, debt securities, and loans (refer to Eurostat, 2013). Note that the values are reported and should be analysed on a consolidated basis when the 'internal' portion of debt held by a unit within the government sector is not included.[13] In addition, the debt measures exclude certain financial instruments, such as financial derivatives or contingent liabilities. The last item may be necessary, although it only consists of potential liabilities. The contingent liabilities are obligations of the government, whose timing and magnitude depend on the occurrence of some uncertain future events outside the government's control (Ceborati, 2008). For example, they may include government guarantees to public–private partnerships, depositors, or other arrangements.

The distinction between gross and net debt is vital for the overall economic interpretation of any relevant fiscal analysis. From the theoretical perspective, it would be suitable to analyse net debt stock (net position), which is the difference between relevant assets and liabilities. However, this broader definition is subject to further uncertainties. It is often difficult to evaluate the price of government assets, and it may not be comparable to the pricing of government liabilities. In addition,

[10] For example, specific levels of a political system of the given country.

[11] For example, many countries do not have state governments.

[12] It is one of the key supranational fiscal regulations in the EU.

[13] Certain items are not available on a consolidated basis. In these cases, it is mentioned in the text.

some portion of the assets is usually illiquid—they cannot be sold promptly. Therefore, gross debt measures are usually examined, and this work follows the practice. According to the International Monetary Fund (IMF, 2014), gross debt includes all liabilities held in debt instruments. The instruments include all financial claims that require future interest and/or principal payments by the debtor to the creditor (ibid.).

2.3 Adverse Effects of Excessive Debt Accumulation

Historically, government debt has played a significant role in the development of modern economies. It has dramatically increased since the Second World War because of various factors. The first-level causes are possibly national preferences or information asymmetry. Accordingly, the upward trend is connected to a given institutional setting. Historically, some portions of debt were created because of wars or political conflicts. However, the trend in the last two decades has diverged from the earlier experience, and many countries are showing peacetime deficits. These are shown to be linked to the expansion of social programmes, unmatched by tax revenue increases (Mussa & Masson, 1995). Moreover, the current deficits could also be seen as a consequence of economic crises. This work examines the last possibility, which occurred after the last financial crisis of 2008–2009 in the Euro Area.

The problems associated with high debt levels are well-known. It should be noted that the debt issues promote negative 'vicious circles' or spirals in the economy. In other words, the effects are self-reinforcing, which makes the effects even more problematic. First, concerns about debt sustainability usually lead to higher country risk premium, which results in higher debt service and capital outflows.[14] Second, it creates a vulnerability in the economy to other shocks, which may promote another type of crisis, for example, a banking crisis. Third, it promotes economic instabilities because of the overall volatility of consumption and investment.[15] Fourth, higher government spending may crowd out private investment.[16] Fifth, the negative externalities may spread out in the case of integrated country groups like the Euro Area. Sixth, high debt service represents an intergenerational burden—making the current generation better off at the cost of the next generation. Lastly, it is associated

[14]These are especially problematic for developing countries.

[15]A high debt burden may provide a strong disincentive to the overall investment or specific consumption.

[16]It is necessary to distinguish between the basic IS-LM model conclusion and other explanations. The basic IS-LM model associates the crowding-out effect with an increase in the overall interest rate in the economy. In reality, the interest rates are significantly manipulated by the central bank. However, the crowding-out effect may also be thought of as a depletion of resources that could have been invested by the private sector. Furthermore, government investment may eliminate some business opportunities or increase the prices of products due to higher demand.

with a loss of policy flexibility when a government cannot afford to raise spending in recessions due to a prohibitively high debt level. As a result, it leads to lower government revenues, a higher chance of default, and lower economic growth. The effect on economic growth has been the subject of various studies and is examined in the following section.

2.3.1 Sovereign Debt and Economic Growth

The economic theory differentiates between three main approaches to the effects of public indebtedness on economic growth. The Neoclassical theory finds the macroeconomic impacts of budget deficit harmful because it promotes economic instabilities. Contrastingly, the Keynesian approach finds the impact to be positive mainly in the cases of low effective aggregate demand. However, Neo-Ricardianism states that there is no impact due to individual rationality (Strecha, 2015).

The evidence and beliefs about the Ricardian equivalence are mixed. Despite its brilliance, the concept does not have a strong theoretical background, especially when considering new insights in behavioural economics made in recent decades. David Ricardo himself did not believe that the theorem holds. In contrast, he supported the debt-illusion explanation (Brennan, 2012). Stanley (1998) concludes in his meta-study that there is no evidence of equivalence. Therefore, the debate is about whether some exceptional circumstances exist, as the Keynesian approach suggests.

Authors who are in favour of indebtedness usually mention its long-term growth effects when making appropriate investments and the fact that in times of crises, depressed economies may need a '*push*'. Unfortunately, there is evidence that profitable investments are rarely made due to the political process, and the resources are usually wasted on political campaigns. The second reason is usually invalid because of its unsustainability and does not focus on the root causes of crises. By postponing a recession, the adverse long-term effects are becoming only worse. The Euro Area and its design is a clear example of the unsoundness of attitude. Hishow (2011) explains the rationality of policymakers' fear of fiscal discipline as they are likely to be punished by voters who lost their jobs in the wake of budget reforms. The fact was strengthened by the design of the Euro Area when the socialisation of risk and losses is possible. Nevertheless, there is no need to eliminate the debt entirely due to costs being prohibitive.[17] As mentioned earlier, the comprehensive studies listed below found the relevant debt-to-GDP ratio threshold between 85% and 100%. It would probably be sufficient for the EU4 countries to comply with the Maastricht criterion of 60% for two reasons. One, it provides a sufficient buffer when an

[17] There is a difference between a 'limited-living' individual and arguably 'infinitely-living' government. However, many of the implications remain similar except for certain thresholds.

economy is having problems. Two, these countries formally pledged to follow the rule.

Gál and Babos (2014) summarise the results of nine comprehensive empirical studies from 2010 to 2013 concerning the impacts of high debt. They recommend that new EU member states avoid high debt levels due to their negative influence on GDP growth and problems connected with deleveraging. All the mentioned papers present adverse growth effects of a high debt-to-GDP ratio (usually between 85% and 100%), with only one exception, the study of Herndon et al. (2013). The authors criticise the well-known work of Reinhart and Rogoff (2010), arguing that the negative effect is not present in every case of high debt. Égert (2015) joins the criticism and mentions lapses in the original study of Rogoff and Reinhart; however, his results also suggest the negative impact of high debt, which is kicking in at already moderate public debt levels in some cases. A newer study by Woo and Kumar (2015) also confirms the hypothesis. The authors claim that there is a slowdown in labour productivity growth mainly due to reduced investment and slower growth of capital per worker. In addition, a state of high debt may not only increase uncertainty in an economy but also raise its vulnerability to crises, leading to higher macroeconomic volatility, as previously mentioned. On the whole, history indicates that episodes of high debt growth in the EU were unsuccessful in the mid-term or the long-term because the resources were usually spent inefficiently.

According to economic theory, and empirical studies, the adverse effects of high debt on GDP growth are indisputable. Nevertheless, the effects are probably different in time and space; they are highly volatile and country-specific.[18] It is also necessary to address the concerns that excessive indebtedness in the Euro Area[19] may be lowered by raising inflation and GDP growth. Output growth usually plays a significant role in determining fiscal balances in both downturn and recovery episodes (Icaza, 2018). Moreover, it increases the country's likelihood of a significant debt reduction (Nickel et al., 2010). Arguably, under the current institutional design of the Euro Area, this is not a viable possibility. On the one hand, the Euro Area countries are among the slowest growing regions in the world (see IMF, 2022). On the other hand, high inflation rates hurt the overall economic health of a country and are usually a sign of significant structural problems in the respective economy.

[18] Advanced economies are able to defy the adverse effects of the burden better than developing economies because of lower risk premium dynamics and better investment environment.

[19] Especially in the EU4 countries.

2.4 Sovereign Debt Sustainability Assessments

An important aspect of fiscal analysis is the long-term view or sustainability evaluation. An unsustainable level[20] of government debt exhibits many adverse effects, including lower GDP growth or lower '*manoeuvring*' space for discretionary fiscal policy, which may ultimately lead to government default. Two essential concepts need to be distinguished, viz: liquidity and solvency. The former is rather short-term oriented, while the latter is used from a long-term perspective. Liquidity is defined as the ability to honour liabilities payable at the current point in time or the ability to roll over the debt. It is often measured by the gross financing needs indicator, which consists of debt service (interest and principal payments) and budget balance at a given time. Solvency means for the country to be able to repay its debt at some point in time fully.

It should be noted that the two concepts are linked together, even though they focus on different time frames. Insolvency necessarily implies illiquidity at some point in time. However, illiquidity does not necessarily imply insolvency—the opposite is not true. Hence, there is an argument for saving an entity that is temporarily illiquid while still solvent. This was the case for some companies during the financial crisis of 2008–2009, and it can also apply to government finance. The notion of sovereign debt sustainability is also connected with the analyses of various risks, including market perception of the sovereign, debt maturity structure, currency composition of the debt, availability of liquid assets, and other factors.

According to Sturzenegger and Zettelmeyer (2007, p. 308): '*debt sustainability is one of the most used and abused concepts in the recent discussions on preventing and resolving sovereign debt crises*'. The reason is that the sustainability of sovereign debt can be defined from various perspectives as it involves many alternative methodologies. Wyplosz (2007, p. 3) states that the sustainability analysis asks the following question: '*When is a country's debt becoming so big that it will not be fully serviced?*' This is possibly the most general definition of debt sustainability; however, it is necessary to be more specific. Debt sustainability is based on the notion of solvency. Economists often derive formal intertemporal solvency conditions, which can be adjusted to imply that the debt cannot exceed the net present or discounted value of future primary surpluses.[21] It imposes a constraint on the government. If the initial debt stock is positive, then the government needs to run primary surpluses in the future.

However, the assumption of an infinite or a very long-time horizon may be overly abstract and subject to significant risks and uncertainties in practice—regarding the future values of interest payments and primary balances. Hence, alternative ways of debt sustainability analysis have been proposed.

---

[20] Similar to unsustainable flows—budget deficits.

[21] The problematics have been described by many authors. Most notably, the IMF has published many manuals and guidelines—see IMF (2013) and Escolano (2010). Moreover, Piscetek (2019) within the New Zealand Treasury provides a clear summary of the problematics.

The formal solvency condition does not state how primary balances should be improved when needed. Arguably, there are appropriate and inappropriate ways to do it (Wyplosz, 2007). For instance, a government default would reduce current liabilities, but it cannot be considered an appropriate solution due to adverse economic effects. The same principle applies to the threat of hyperinflation. Furthermore, it is necessary to consider the potential political feasibility of sustainability adjustments and the realism of macroeconomic assumptions regarding sustainability evaluation. As a result, debt sustainability analysis necessarily involves probabilistic judgments, including the possible occurrence of economic shocks. In this context, the sustainability concept is significantly more demanding than the pure concept of solvency (ibid.).

Therefore, the IMF uses a different definition that incorporates all the requirements. The institution defines that '*a sovereign debt can be regarded as sustainable when the primary balance needed to at least stabilize debt under both the baseline and realistic shock scenarios is economically and politically feasible,*[22] *such that the level of debt is consistent with an acceptably low rollover risk and with preserving potential growth at a satisfactory level*'[23] (IMF, 2013, p. 4). In other words, the assessment focuses on the debt level and its trajectory, feasibility of the fiscal adjustment, debt profile, and rollover risks. As mentioned, the assessment needs to examine the country's capacity to repay the debt. Hence, I also examine the relevant GDP ratios in the following text. An alternative approach claims that the debt is unsustainable if projected debt ratios either increase or remain high (Piscetek, 2019). However, this definition may neglect important details.

Finally, many of the approaches to debt sustainability evaluation are based on a relatively static view (partial equilibrium principles) because the forecasts are subject to significant uncertainty. The dynamic relationships between the examined variables are not considered. However, fiscal policy affects the economic environment and vice versa.

Considering all the facts, this work presents an analysis based on various approaches. These include theoretical mechanisms, descriptive statistics of relevant fiscal variables, traditional analysis of fiscal efforts and positions, debt projections based on the framework of debt dynamics, and the feasibility of various approaches to sovereign debt reduction of the EU4 countries.

References

Barhoumi, K., Cherif, R., & Rebei, N. (2018). Stochastic trends and fiscal policy. *Economic Modelling, 75*, 256–267. https://doi.org/10.1016/j.econmod.2018.06.024

Barwell, R. (2016). *Macroeconomic policy after the crash*. Palgrave Macmillan. https://doi.org/10.1057/978-1-137-51592-6. ISBN: 978-1-137-51591-9.

[22]It means that unrealistically large adjustments from both perspectives are not being considered.

[23]These other requirements imply that the government should not default.

Brennan, G. (2012). The political economy of public debt. *Constitutional Political Economy, 23*(3), 182–198. https://doi.org/10.1007/s10602-012-9124-5

Bloch, D., & Fall, F. (2015). *Government debt indicators: Understanding the data* (OECD Economics Department Working Paper No. 1228). Organisation for Economic Co-Operation and Development (OECD). Retrieved July 17, 2022, from https://www.oecd-ilibrary.org/economics/government-debt-indicators_5jrxv0ftbff2-en

Cangiano, M., & Mottu, E. (1998). *Will fiscal policy be effective under EMU* (IMF Working Paper No. 98/176). International Monetary Fund. Retrieved July 17, 2022, from https://www.imf.org/external/pubs/ft/wp/wp98176.pdf

Cottarelli, C., Gerson, P., & Senhadji, A. (2014). *Post-crisis fiscal policy*. The MIT Press. ISBN: 978-0262027182.

Ceborati, A. (2008). *Contingent liabilities: Issues and practice* (IMF Working Paper No. 08/245). International Monetary Fund. Retrieved July 17, 2022, from https://www.imf.org/external/pubs/ft/wp/2008/wp08245.pdf

Égert, B. (2015). The 90% public debt threshold: The rise and fall of a stylized fact. *Applied Economics, 47*(34–35), 3756–3770. https://doi.org/10.1080/00036846.2015.1021463

Escolano, J. (2010). *A practical guide to public debt dynamics, fiscal sustainability, and cyclical adjustment of budgetary aggregates* (Technical Note and Manual No. 2010/02). International Monetary Fund. Retrieved May 28, 2022, from https://www.imf.org/external/pubs/ft/tnm/2010/tnm1002.pdf

Eurostat. (2022). *Eurostat Database*. Retrieved September 21, 2022, from https://ec.europa.eu/eurostat

Eurostat. (2016). *Manual on Government Deficit and Debt Implementation of ESA 2010: 2016 Edition*. Publications Office of the European Union. ISBN: 978-92-79-55319-6.

Eurostat. (2013). *European System of Accounts: ESA 2010* (Manual and Guideline KS-02-13-269-EN-C). European Union. https://doi.org/10.2785/16644

Gál, Z., & Babos, P. (2014). Avoiding the high debt – low growth trap: Lessons for the new member states. *Business Systems & Economics, 4*(2), 154–167. https://doi.org/10.13165/vse-14-4-2-04

Herndon, T., Ash, M., & Pollin, R. (2013). Does high public debt consistently stifle economic growth? A critique of Reinhart and Rogoff. *Cambridge Journal of Economics, 38*(2), 257–279. https://doi.org/10.1093/cje/bet075

Hishow, O. N. (2011). Germany's debt brake: Pulling the EU out of its debt trap? *Intereconomics, 46*(6), 327–331. https://doi.org/10.1007/s10272-011-0396-1

International Monetary Fund (IMF). (2022). *World Economic Outlook Database*. Retrieved August 15, 2022, from https://www.imf.org/en/Publications/WEO

International Monetary Fund (IMF). (2014). *Public sector debt statistics: Guide for compilers and users*. International Monetary Fund. https://doi.org/10.5089/9781484378991.069. ISBN: 978-1-61635-156-4.

International Monetary Fund. (2013). *Staff guidance note for public debt sustainability analysis in market-access countries* (Tech. Rep.). International Monetary Fund. Retrieved May 28, 2022, from https://www.imf.org/external/np/pp/eng/2013/050913.pdf

Icaza, V. E. (2018). Fiscal fatigue and debt sustainability: Empirical evidence from the Eurozone 1980–2013. *Cuadernos de Economia, 41*(115), 69–78. https://doi.org/10.1016/j.cesjef.2017.03.002

Langdana, F. K. (2016). *Macroeconomic policy: Demystifying monetary and fiscal policy*. Springer International Publishing. https://doi.org/10.1007/978-3-319-32854-6. ISBN: 978-3-319-32852-2.

Mussa, M., & Masson, P. R. (1995). *Long-term tendencies in budget deficits and debt* (IMF Working Paper No. 95/128). International Monetary Fund. Retrieved July 10, 2022, from https://www.imf.org/en/Publications/WP/Issues/2016/12/30/Long-Term-Tendencies-in-Budget-Deficits-and-Debt-1957

Nickel, C., Rother, P., & Zimmermann, L. (2010). *Major public debt reductions: Lessons from the past, lessons for the future* (ECB Working Paper No. 1241). European Central Bank. Retrieved July 10, 2022, from https://www.ecb.europa.eu/pub/pdf/scpwps/ecbwp1241.pdf

Piscetek, M. (2019). *Public debt dynamics in New Zealand* (Working Paper No. 19/01). New Zealand Treasury. Retrieved May 28, 2022, from https://treasury.govt.nz/sites/default/files/2019-07/twp19-01.pdf

Reinhart, C. M., & Rogoff, K. S. (2010). Growth in a time of debt. *American Economic Review, 100*(2), 573–578. https://doi.org/10.1257/aer.100.2.573

Stanley, T. D. (1998). New wine in old bottles: A meta-analysis of Ricardian equivalence. *Southern Economic Journal, 64*(3), 713–727. http://www.jstor.org/stable/1060788

Strecha, M. (2015). Public debt structure as an origin of economic instability. *Actual Problems in Economics, 2*(164), 328–338. https://bit.ly/2ZhVfaR

Sturzenegger, F., & Zettelmeyer, J. (2007). *Debt defaults and lessons from a decade of crises*. MIT Press. https://doi.org/10.7551/mitpress/2295.001.0001. ISBN: 978-02-62-19553-9.

Vebrová, L., & Rybáček, V. (2014). How to read government deficit and debt. *Statistics and Economy Journal, 94*(3), 32–46. https://www.czso.cz/documents/10180/25609548/32019714q3032.pdf/fac30b6b-238f-4d77-8149-9b1f614abedd?version=1.0

Woo, J., & Kumar, M. S. (2015). Public debt and growth. *Economica, 82*(328), 705–739. https://doi.org/10.1111/ecca.12138

Wyplosz, C. (2007). *Debt sustainability assessment: The IMF approach and alternatives* (IHEID Working Paper No. 03/2007). The Graduate Institute of International Studies. https://ideas.repec.org/p/gii/giihei/heiwp03-2007.html

Chapter 3
European Debt Crisis and Flaws of the Euro Area

This chapter focuses on a brief description of the European debt crisis and the relevant economic policy implications. The second main theme is an identification of structural flaws of the Euro Area, which lead to the unfavourable situation of the EU4 countries.

3.1 Causes and Implications of the European Debt Crisis

A sovereign debt crisis[1] can be defined as government default, involuntary debt restructuring, or belief that this is about to occur. It is often combined with a banking crisis (Reinhart & Rogoff, 2013). Furthermore, it is appropriate to distinguish between internal and external debt crises. The latter case can be more strongly accompanied by '*sudden stops*' following a capital inflows episode. However, the distinction is more problematic in the Euro Area due to the sharing of risks. The mechanism of a sovereign debt crisis is illustrated in Fig. 3.1.

The previous financial crisis of 2008–2009, which provided the impetus for the European debt crisis, should be distinguished into two phases. It is well-known that in 2006, the US real estate house prices bubble burst, and soon after that, the US banking sector collapsed. One of the milestones was the failure of Lehman Brothers on 15 September 2008. The US crisis was a result of multiple causes. However, the primary reasons were arguably sub-optimal economic policies that promoted economic instabilities. These included prohibitively expansionary fiscal and monetary policies combined with inappropriate regulations. Two regulatory measures, the Housing for Everyone initiative (Housing and Community Development Act) and

[1]The European debt crisis is often also referred to as the eurozone crisis or the European sovereign debt crisis. Note that the level of government debt is both the cause and the consequence of the problems in the Euro Area.

M. Bednář, *Fiscal Policy in the Southern European Union Countries*, Contributions to Finance and Accounting, https://doi.org/10.1007/978-3-031-29761-8_3

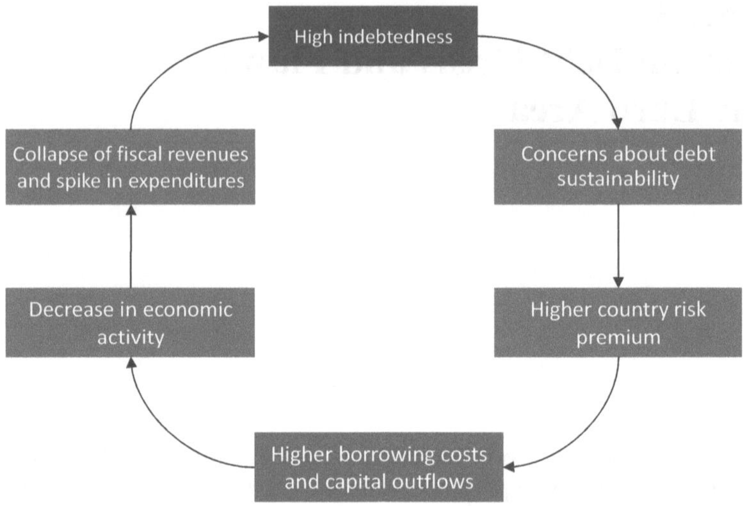

Fig. 3.1 Vicious debt circle mechanism. Source: Own processing

significant deregulation in the financial sector (Gramm–Leach–Bliley Act) were crucial. Both legislative packages were promoted in the era of the 42nd US President Bill Clinton in the 1990s.

The second phase was the transmission of the financial crisis to Europe through banking sector linkages. The crisis uncovered deep structural flaws in the Euro Area as the most fragile Southern European countries were hit the hardest. Moreover, it showed that government bonds could not be considered strictly safe assets. The causes of the sovereign debt crisis in the Euro Area are connected to its institutional flaws and the inability to fulfil the OCA criteria by many countries.[2] In total, eight EU countries received financial help (explicit bail-out[3]) through various rescue mechanisms. Italy was the only EU4 country that did not receive any help. Spain received 41 billion euros between 2012 and 2014, Portugal 78 billion euros between 2011 and 2014, and Greece approximately 257 billion euros between 2010 and 2018 (see European Commission, 2022a). It should be noted that Article 125 of the Lisbon Treaty contained a 'no-bail-out clause'. The regulation was violated.

Furthermore, the EU devised a '*rescue plan*' called the Next Generation EU package to respond to the COVID-19 pandemic. The plan amounted to 750 billion euros in 2018 prices, and the funds are being borrowed by the EU, which is directly connected to the socialisation of risks. Moreover, the funds from the Recovery and Resilience Facility, which account for the vast majority of the financial

[2] Most prominently, these are the EU4 countries. It is discussed in detail in a separate section in this chapter.

[3] The term 'bail-out' refers to external financial help.

disbursements from the Next-Generation EU package, are targeted mainly to Italy, Spain, and France.[4]

Evidently, the European debt crisis did not end because the structural problems and the accumulated debts of the EU4 countries were not eliminated. The expansionary policy of the ECB helped mitigate the worst short- and mid-term effects, but it was unable (by definition) to solve the issues.

Currently, two main approaches used to deal with the situation can be identified. The first approach is considered the current political mainstream and is based on federalist ideology. The approach arguably does not offer any sound economic solutions. It focuses on 'repairing' the existing structural issues but does not deal with their causes. It is connected to various propositions, including promoting fiscal discipline, political unification, establishing a fiscal union, and other factors. The second approach is based on the idea of intergovernmentalism, which follows a sound economic theory connected to the Optimum Currency Area (OCA) Theory.[5] The approach focuses on the causes of structural inefficiencies and identifies significant heterogeneity among the EU countries. As a result, the proposed solutions are less ambitious and focus on restructuring the Euro Area regarding its country composition.

3.1.1 *Implicit Bail-Out Mechanism*

Many economists are aware of a possible implicit bail-out mechanism. The issue was initially identified and discussed by German economist and President of the Ifo Institute for Economic Research at that time, Hans-Werner Sinn (2012). Figure 3.2 shows the TARGET2[6] balances for the EU4 countries as of December of each year.

The net borrowers consisted primarily of Germany, Ireland, and Luxembourg. These three countries accounted for approximately 93% of the total borrower position value as of December 2021. At the same time, Germany alone accounted for more than 70% of the total value. Furthermore, the data show that (approximately) since the financial crisis of 2008–2009, all the EU4 countries are net lenders, which is represented by negative values. The EU4 countries accounted for approximately 88% of the total lender position value (excluding the ECB) as of December 2021. The values for the EU4 countries show double-digit percentages of the respective GDP ratios.

There are multiple causes of the occurrence, including comparatively higher risk premiums of the countries, significant structural inefficiencies, lack of profitable investment opportunities, and other factors. The movements demonstrate a 'capital

[4]These countries' maximum financial contributions make up more than 50% of the total funds as of June 2022 (see European Commission, 2022b).

[5]The OCA Theory is explained later in this chapter.

[6]TARGET2 is a real-time gross settlement system owned and operated by the Eurosystem.

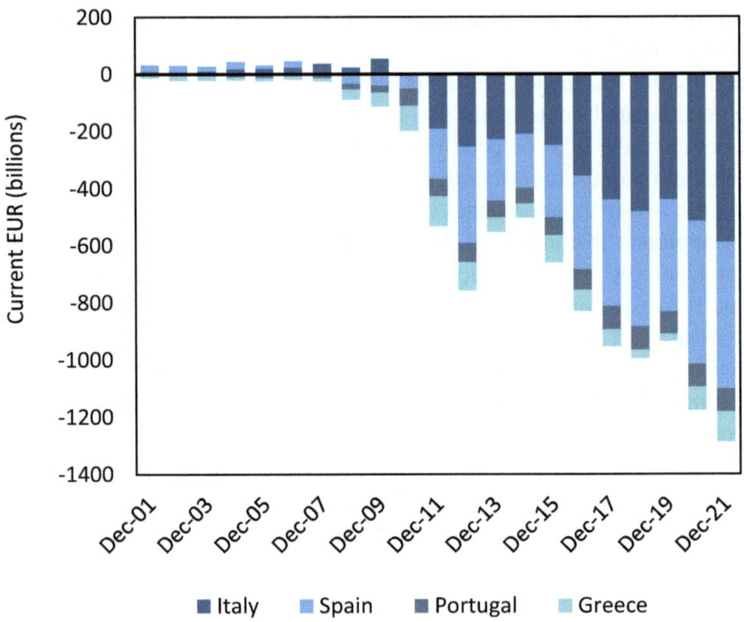

Fig. 3.2 TARGET2 (im)balances—EU4, 2001–2021. Note: The data show current prices because it is unclear which deflator to use. Moreover, the inclusion of current prices does not bias the general trends and implications. Source: Institute of Empirical Economic Research (2022), own processing

flight' from the Southern countries to the Northern or core countries of the EU (see Cheung et al., 2020). The ECB (2016) attributed the movements to the redistribution effects of its quantitative easing programmes. However, Minenna et al. (2018) showed that the explanation is inconsistent for Italy and Spain. The authors claim that the deterioration in the countries' balances is mainly due to a shift of private-sector financial wealth from government securities to foreign assets—the capital flight.

The implicit bail-out mechanism is illustrated in Fig. 3.3. Note the dashed line coming from the Greek Central Bank to the ECB. In some cases, the Greek Central Bank does not have enough monetary reserves; hence the ECB plays a guarantor role. The ECB creates monetary reserves on its own and provides them to the German Central Bank, and later, they are credited to the exporter's commercial bank account. Therefore, the ECB has outstanding claims on future Greek reserves. The implicit bail-out will occur if these claims are not paid. The emission of new reserves will ultimately be 'paid' by the Euro Area citizens in the form of 'unfair' and inefficient redistribution effects and higher inflation. Furthermore, the interest rate policy of the ECB does not consider the intrinsic country risks of the EU4; it is lending them very '*cheaply*'.

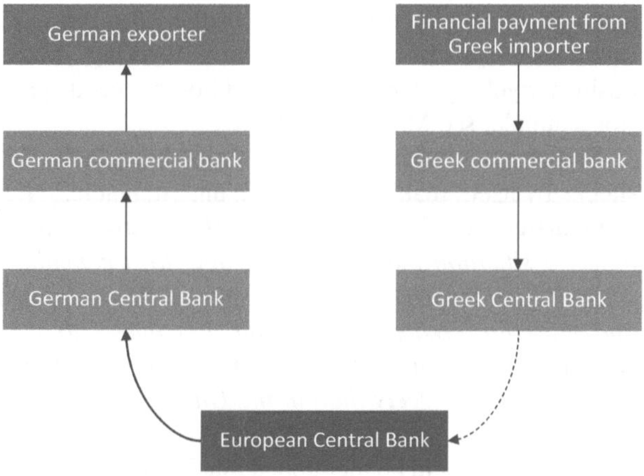

Fig. 3.3 Chain of transactions in the TARGET2 System—example of Greek importer and German exporter. Source: Own processing

Table 3.1 Optimum Currency Area theory—main criteria

A. Mechanisms to deal with asymmetric shocks	B. Characteristics that help absorb asymmetric shocks
1. Labour and capital flexibility (or wage and price flexibility)	3. Production diversification
2. Fiscal transfers	4. Economic openness
	5. Business cycle synchronisation
	6. Homogeneous preferences

Source: Broz (2005) and Kunroo (2015), own adjustments and processing

3.2 Optimum Currency Area Theory

To be able to perform a positive economic analysis of the Euro Area, a theoretical framework, which fits the purpose, needs to be employed. In the 1960s, Mundell (1961) pioneered the concept of the OCA Theory. Later, the theory was further developed by other economists. The most notable contributions include the works of McKinnon (1963) and Kenen (1969).

The OCA theory can be used to evaluate whether a particular monetary union (common currency area) meets the requirements for its efficient functioning. The framework cannot provide a definitive answer because some viable assumptions are qualitative and normative, for instance, political issues. Nevertheless, the OCA Theory can analyse and evaluate the necessary requirements. Table 3.1 summarises the essential criteria.[7]

The central argument is that the member countries within a monetary union should be as homogeneous as possible. The problem is when the group is relatively

[7] The list of all the possible criteria would be significantly longer. For instance, refer to Broz (2005, p. 72). However, the presented list focuses only on the essentials for a transparent and coherent analysis.

heterogeneous, which is the case of the Euro Area. The mechanisms to deal with asymmetric shocks are not properly working. Moreover, the Euro Area lacks business cycle synchronisation[8] and homogeneous preferences among the countries (for example, see Monteverdi, 2016).

Furthermore, when a monetary union has a faulty design, it produces asymmetric shocks by itself, making the system unsustainable.[9] Nobel laureate Milton Friedman summarised the situation in 1997: '*By contrast, Europe's common market exemplifies a situation that is unfavourable to a common currency. It is composed of separate nations whose residents speak different languages, have different customs, and have far greater loyalty and attachment to their own country than to the common market or to the idea of "Europe". Despite being a free trade area, goods move less freely than in the United States, and so does capital.*' (Friedman, 1997, p. 2).

Finally, it should be mentioned that Frankel and Rose (1998) proposed the idea of OCA endogeneity. It states that fulfilling the criteria may not be necessary because membership in the Euro Area may adjust the country's characteristics to fit the criteria over time. The argument is possibly correct for international trade, but it is insufficient. According to the real data, the Euro Area likely did not promote homogeneity over the years (Eurostat, 2022).[10] In fact, the previous financial and COVID-19 crises have furthered the discrepancies among the countries, as the EU4 countries were hit the most. The following text provides a detailed overview of the Euro Area's issues.

3.3 Systemic Flaws of the Euro Area

Statistical evidence shows that the dynamics of general government gross debt are significantly different between countries within and outside the Euro Area. According to Coccia (2018), the economic policy within the Euro Area is deteriorating and increasing the member countries' sovereign debts and fiscal deficits. Therefore, the following text focuses on the analysis of the possible factors. The cause of almost all the issues is the heterogeneity of the countries combined with the results of normative political ideologies. The EU and Euro Area are countries with different cultures, interests, opinions, and policies. Nevertheless, the establishment of the common currency is not a fundamentally flawed project. The Euro Area is not sustainable only under the current policies and country composition.

[8]The measurement of this criterion is problematic. A simple correlation is not sufficient. Arguably, the analysis needs to be conducted in a time-frequency domain. For example, by using a wavelet framework.

[9]This issue is discussed in the next chapter, using an example of fiscal centralisation.

[10]Refer to the basic macroeconomic variables of the EU19, which are provided by Eurostat (2022). For a detailed discussion, refer to Mody (2018) or Loužek (2015).

3.3.1 *Overly Ambitious Integration Ideology*

There has been a strong emphasis on deeper integration within the EU over the years.[11] The idea was put forward by Germany and France, two of the most powerful countries that are, arguably, trying to control the integration as much as possible and gain benefits. The benefits are not necessarily in a monetary form. The countries are net payers to the EU's common budget; however, they can significantly influence decision-making processes within the EU and the Euro Area.

Their abilities have been reinforced by the Lisbon Treaty of 2009, which gave more power to richer and larger countries.[12] The central argument of this part is that the more specific policies or regulatory burdens a policymaker implements, the more likely it is that the measures will not fit all countries. It creates both economic and political tensions within the integration process. The political tensions are directly observable as there is a lack of homogeneous preferences among the countries.[13]

Furthermore, even if there was a perfect homogeneity of preferences, it is impossible to follow strictly political and normative ideology without some level of economic alignment. Sooner or later, the economic issues arising from the mismatch between ideology and reality manifest and create significant instabilities, which also shape the political sphere.

3.3.2 *Country Composition of the Euro Area*

Political decisions should always follow the economic fundamentals, at least to some extent. The Euro Area, arguably, consists of some countries that should not be its members. For example, it is widely known that Greece falsified some of its statistics to be able to join the Euro Area in 2001 (see Berend, 2017). These lapses in the country composition of the Euro Area have manifested during the various EU crises.[14]

[11]For instance, refer to the historical statements of French President Emmanuel Macron or German Chancellor Angela Merkel.

[12]This is apparent when analysing the voting process and voting weights of the countries in the Council of the European Union. The EU representatives used the argument that this is for the sake of efficiency in the voting process. The processes are now arguably more efficient but at the expense of the sovereignty of smaller countries.

[13]This statement is very thoroughly supported by evidence. Refer to the previous discussions about the common agricultural policy, common asylum policy of the EU, the debate about the coronavirus financial packages, green policies, energy policies linked to Russia, and other issues.

[14]For instance, these include the financial crisis of 2008–2009, European debt crisis, migration crisis, and COVID-19 crisis.

Fig. 3.4 Effects of the common currency in less competitive countries. Note: This figure is a simplification. Many transmission channels and ambiguous effects are neglected. Refer to the text below. Source: Own processing

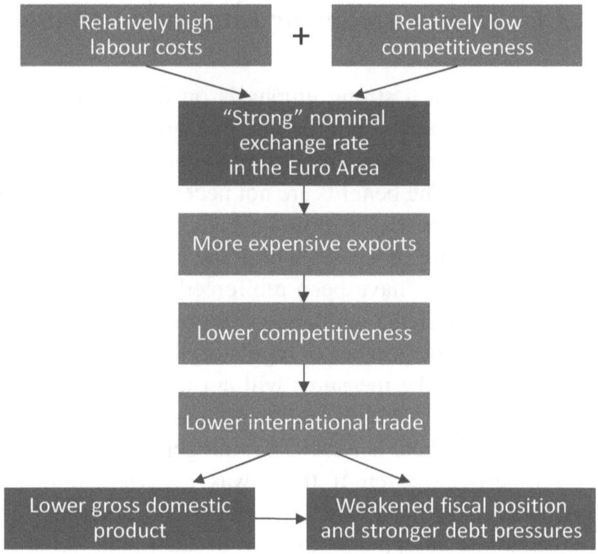

The central issue is that the main parameters of the common currency in the Euro Area simply do not fit all the countries.[15] This is the case of the uniform interest rate set by the ECB and, most notably, the euro currency exchange rate.[16] Economists consider the exchange rate to be one of the essential prices in an economy. It acts as a vital balancing mechanism in the economy; it helps align external demand with internal supply and vice versa. Nevertheless, the balancing mechanism cannot properly work when the Euro Area countries share a uniform exchange rate and the monetary union has inadequate country composition.

It is possible to identify countries for which the uniform exchange rate is 'overly strong'. These are, most notably, the EU4 countries that show lower economic performance and overall competitiveness. When an exchange rate shows real appreciation, it usually leads to lower competitiveness of a country because its exports are '*more expensive*'.[17] The effects of the common currency on the less competitive countries in the Euro Area are illustrated in Fig. 3.4. However, note that the diagram

[15] This argument was strengthened in recent years by implementing various political decisions regarding the socialisation of risks in the EU. The argument was also mentioned by Feldstein (2012).

[16] Some people are still confused by the regime of the euro currency. Even though the euro follows a flexible (floating) exchange rate regime, it is not the case for smaller countries. For instance, Portugal cannot significantly influence the exchange rate on its own due to its relatively smaller economy accompanied by comparatively lower international trade flows. This fact means that Portugal is following a relatively fixed exchange rate regime. The resulting euro exchange rate level and its changes can be seen as a '*weighted average*', where the weights are international trade flows of the member countries.

[17] It can be argued that imports are '*cheaper*', but their significance is usually much lower. Export performance is connected to domestic companies that provide employment.

is a simplification. It neglects many channels and dynamic relationships, most notably the role of the inflation rate.

If the other balancing mechanisms are weak, the disproportionate functioning of the exchange rate mechanism may lead to higher inflation and internal devaluation, which should lower real labour costs and promote competitiveness. However, the devaluation may also lead to lower wages, which decrease aggregate demand, GDP, and competitiveness due to the sub-optimal allocation of production factors and resources. In addition, the effects of artificially low interest rates kept by the ECB and budget deficits offset the mechanism. For example, Baumgarten and Klodt (2010), and Stiglitz (2016) provide a detailed discussion.

As a result, the EU4 economies are permanently destabilised while functioning less efficiently at the same time. In the case of a significant economic shock, the financial crisis of 2008–2009 or the recent coronavirus crisis, a vicious (self-reinforcing) circle of a decline in competitiveness occurs. There is never a '*free lunch*' in economic matters, and the same notion applies to macroeconomic transmission channels. Hence, the exchange rate channel is partly blocked as the common currency cannot properly depreciate and reflect the country's macroeconomic performance. It leads to lower GDP through the income channel, which may also be accompanied by higher debt pressures, internal devaluations, and capital outflows.

Furthermore, economic recovery mechanisms are also working inefficiently. Many economists have not recognised this fact. The EU4 countries still struggle to reach robust and sustainable economic growth. The main lesson is that the economic stability loss from the foregoing exchange rates and national monetary policies is possibly greater than monetary efficiency gains (see Jager & Hafner, 2013).

3.3.3 The Common Monetary Policy Under Fiscal Dominance

The standard notion is that monetary authority (central bank) aims to influence inflation[18] while fiscal authority (usually a government) controls government debt through budget balances. However, when a country shows high government debt levels, then the central bank assumes a somewhat more dominant position to confront the fiscal problem (Afonso et al., 2019). Hence, there is evidence of a substitutional relationship between the two macroeconomic policies. However, the ECB in the Euro Area is aware of the issue and is arguably caught up in the so-called fiscal dominance environment where it cannot act independently.

On the one hand, the effects were pronounced by the policy of quantitative easing. The policy implies redistributive effects as the ECB buys large amounts of private and public financial instruments so that its balance sheet increases

[18] A more accurate term is '*rate of price level change*'. Nevertheless, the term '*inflation rate*' or '*inflation*' is considered a standard in economic literature.

significantly. On the other hand, the effects are more complicated in the Euro Area due to the common currency. It creates a variety of interactions across countries due to country-specific fiscal policies (ibid.). In an ideal scenario, both macroeconomic policies should create an 'optimal policy mix', but it is often not the case in practice. Regarding the examined topic, the text examines the case when monetary policy influences fiscal policy. Arguably, this channel is more robust, while the inverse causality is not relevant to the topic of this work.

In general, monetary policy influences four main types of variables relevant to fiscal policy: economic growth, interest rates, price level measures, and exchange rates. The standard economic theory suggests that expansive monetary policy lowers nominal and real interest rates[19]—contributing to a more favourable fiscal position.[20] Lower interest rates thus usually boost economic growth, which may stimulate inflation.[21] Furthermore, lower interest rates usually lead to exchange rate depreciation through the uncovered interest parity mechanism.[22] The depreciation may stimulate economic growth through higher net exports, provided that the Marshall–Lerner condition[23] is satisfied.

Nevertheless, the effect of depreciation may be ambiguous because it raises the value of debt denominated in foreign currencies.[24] The exchange rate channel is functioning only partially in the Euro Area, meaning that the changes in the exchange rate are not fully country-specific and can be seen as a 'weighted average' of all the Euro Area countries, where the weights are economic positions or significance of the countries in foreign trade. Arguably, the channel also contributes to the relaxed fiscal conditions in the Euro Area due to the expansive monetary policy of the ECB.

In short, the current expansive monetary policy of the ECB contributes to relaxed fiscal conditions and improved budget balances.[25] It helps to make the current fiscal situation of some countries sustainable. However, it brings adverse effects in the

---

[19] It may not apply to a long-term interest rate, which could be higher due to inflation expectations.

[20] However, note that these are rather short-term effects. Monetary policy cannot solve structural problems in the economy.

[21] Inflation can lower the real value of debts; however, this channel is arguably weak in the presented mechanism.

[22] Exchange rate movements compensate for the interest rate differences. In this case, investors are shifting funds out of domestic assets to foreign assets because those offer a higher return. This approach is widely used in general equilibrium models. Nevertheless, note that this is the traditional balance of payments (flow) approach. In contrast, the old monetary approach provides the opposite conclusion. It claims that decreased interest rate would appreciate the domestic currency because it would raise the domestic speculative demand for money, decrease domestic prices, and decrease imports (Jimoh, 2004).

[23] The absolute sum of the country's price elasticities of demand for imports and exports must be higher than one. The condition is usually satisfied in the long term.

[24] However, this is not the case for the EU4 countries because they hold negligible levels of foreign currency-denominated debts. It is shown in the seventh chapter.

[25] Fiscal conditions are relaxed through lower interest rates, while budget balances are improved through higher revenues and lower expenditures.

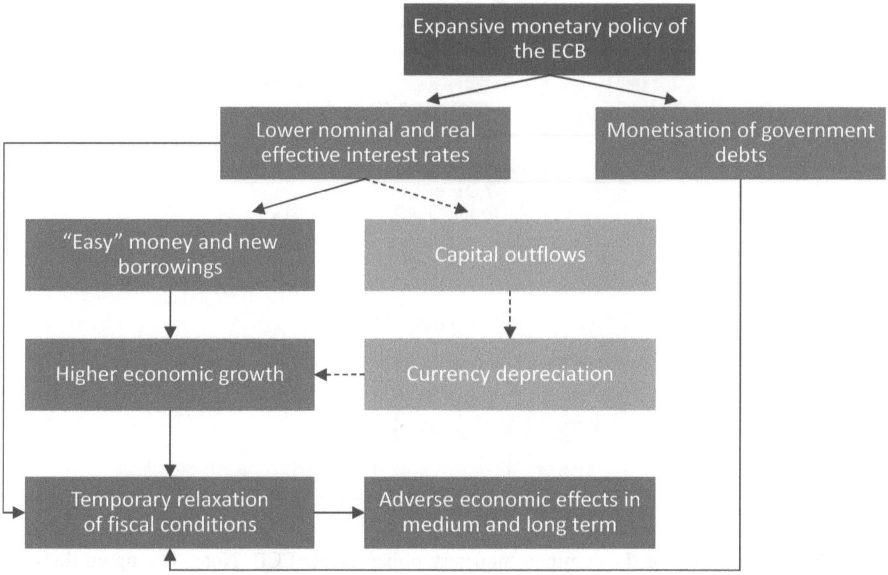

Fig. 3.5 Common monetary policy of the ECB and its effects. Note: This figure is a simplification. Some transmission channels and ambiguous effects are neglected because they are not relevant. Refer to the text above. Source: Own processing

medium and long term.[26] In general, the common monetary policy of the ECB exacerbates the economic and structural inefficiencies in the Euro Area. The precise mechanism is described in the third chapter. Furthermore, the current monetary policy of the ECB also quietly monetises the government debts—lowering them directly.[27] The approach is also associated with prohibitively high adverse effects in the medium and long term. The effects of the common monetary policy in the Euro Area on the country-specific fiscal policies are summarised in Fig. 3.5.

The independence of a central bank is considered an essential characteristic of the current central banking because of historical evidence of fraud in the form of government debt monetisation, which was linked to high inflation.[28] The following text elaborates on the argumentation of Wyplosz (2016), who claims that the situation in the Euro Area is complicated because the ECB currently governs 19 constituencies[29] that have different views of what the central bank should do and their interests often clash with one another. Various EU policies are a result of

[26]Hence, the term 'there is no *free lunch*' was first used in 1942 by Paul Mallon, an American political journalist.

[27]If you are interested in this issue, refer to the discussion and primary and secondary market bond purchases.

[28]High inflation can be seen as a form of an implicit tax burden or as a demonstration of sub-optimal spending, which promotes economic inefficiencies.

[29]The Euro Area will consist of 20 member states as of January 2023—Croatia will be included.

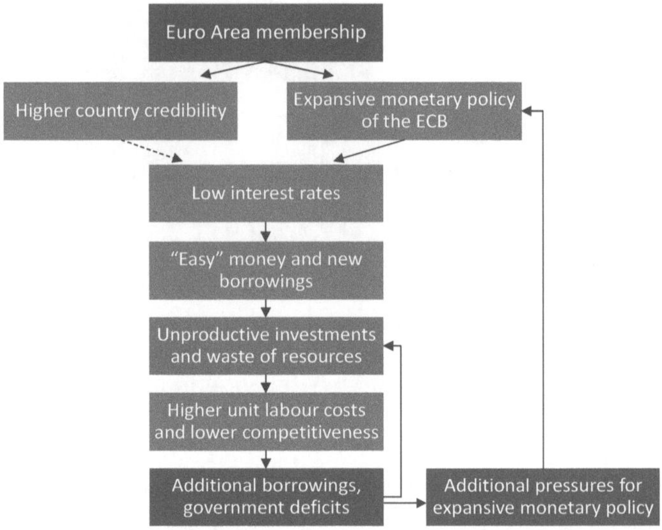

Fig. 3.6 Vicious circle of the common monetary policy of the ECB. Note: The figure does not claim that all the new borrowings are wasted. It describes only one of the possible macroeconomic mechanisms. Source: Own processing

political compromises; hence, the EU legislation consists of many exceptions accompanied by country-specific opt-outs. The situation is even more complicated when the system is fundamentally unstable.

The policy of the ECB cannot be independent when the system needs constant interventions to function. This is a result of a political ideology. Therefore, the ECB is dependent on these circumstances by definition. Moreover, the common monetary policy cannot solve the structural defects. It can only mitigate adverse short-term effects. The policy of the ECB is directly connected to the problems with the composition of the monetary union. The mechanism is illustrated in Fig. 3.6.

Inadequately low (non-equilibrium) interest rates imply substantial borrowing motivations influenced by the idea that 'we should borrow while it is cheap'. These borrowings then may lead to profitable investments under the current policies and EU regulations. Nevertheless, some of them are, in fact, unproductive.[30] Furthermore, it supports moral hazard, which further reinforces the adverse mechanism.

Unproductive investments should lead to higher borrowing costs (higher interest rates). However, the common monetary policy of the ECB does not let such occur. The reason is, again, political. Higher borrowing costs would lead to a major deterioration of the situation of some economies (mainly the EU4 countries).

[30]The other possibility is that investors are motivated to make riskier investments (or even speculations) due to low interest rates in the economy. Arguably, the fact also promotes economic instabilities.

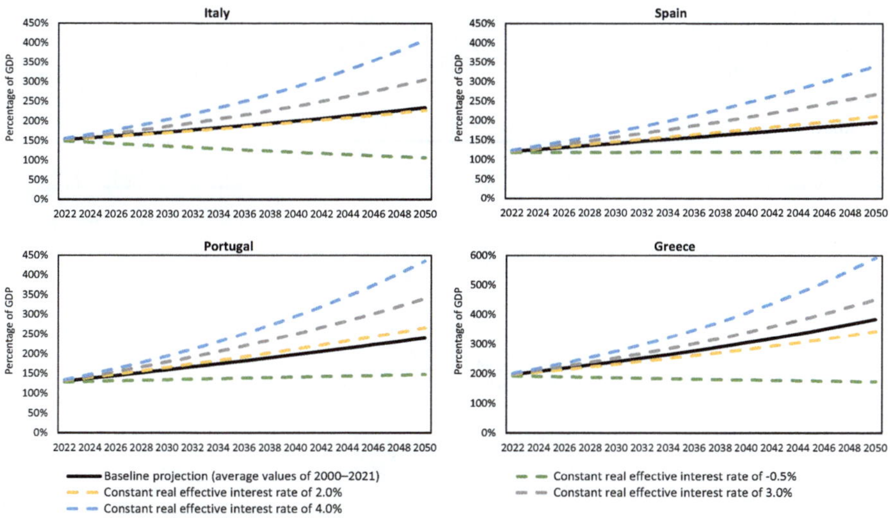

Fig. 3.7 Sensitivity analysis—impact of real effective interest rates on government gross debt to GDP ratios—EU4, 2022–2050. Note: The estimates are based on debt dynamics equations and assumptions of the development of future values according to their 2000–2021 averages. The procedure and related assumptions are presented in the seventh chapter. Source: Own calculations and processing

Unfortunately, a different result is arguably not politically feasible under the current mainstream ideology of the EU.

Finally, a sensitivity analysis is provided in Fig. 3.7. The individual graphs show the possible developments of general government gross consolidated debts of the EU4 countries, under the assumption of average 2000–2021 values of relevant indicators, concerning different real interest rates. On average, the real interest rates of the EU4 countries were historically close to 2%. Hence, the yellow line is close to the baseline projections. However, even a 1 percentage point increase in the rates (i.e. 3% real effective interest rates) would result in drastically higher debt levels in the EU4 countries. For instance, the respective debt ratios of Italy, Spain, Portugal, and Greece would be higher by more than 70, 50, 70, and 100 percentage points, respectively, when compared to the effect of the 2% real effective interest rate by the year 2050. The most affected or the most sensitive country to the interest rate effects is Greece, followed by Italy, Portugal, and Spain.

3.3.4 *Socialisation of Risks and Moral Hazard*

In the past, a large number of financial bail-outs occurred during and in the aftermath of the 2008–2009 financial crisis. This led to a widespread moral hazard among the countries. It was especially the case of the EU4 countries, which were able to

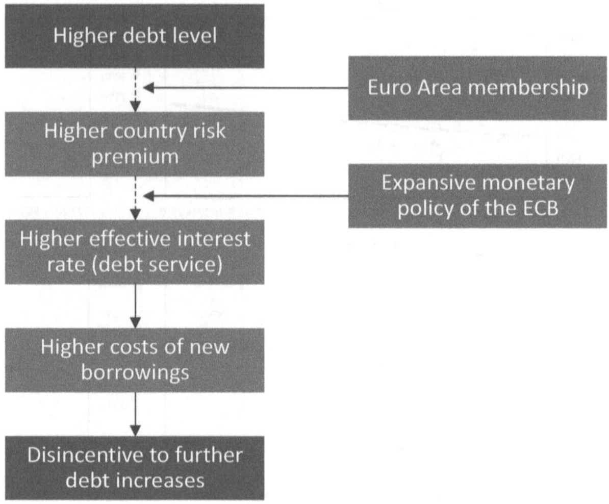

Fig. 3.8 Relationship between the level of debt and fiscal discipline in the Euro Area (disruption of the standard interest rate pass-through). Source: Own processing

significantly boost their spending before the financial crisis due to low interest rates.[31] Hence, one of the main problems regarding fiscal discipline in the Euro Area is the risk-sharing combined with expansive monetary policies of the ECB and lack of fiscal discipline.[32]

Relatively high interest rates should not necessarily be considered a problem. They have a disciplining effect on the behaviour of economic agents, including the government. If this were the case, the EU4 countries would, arguably, not destabilise their economies through significant deficits. Nevertheless, the Euro Area membership and the expansionary policies of the ECB promote low interest rates and the so-called socialisation of risks. Figure 3.8 illustrates the issue. The dashed lines denote weakened or even non-existing effects.

Finally, the Eurosystem does not distinguish between the riskiness of government securities. The EU4 and non-EU4 debt securities are equally accepted as collateral, pushing the socialisation of risks even further. Ultimately, the costs of macroeconomic instabilities and deficits in one of the Euro Area countries are undertaken by all users of the euro currency in the form of reduced purchasing power of the euro currency, lower economic and social welfare, and higher economic instabilities.

[31] However, these were mostly short-term gains. The costs significantly outweigh the benefits in the long run. This '*irrationality*' may be partly attributed to the political process and its cycles.

[32] One of the fiscal '*solutions*' is usually considered the establishment of a fiscal union. The issue is analysed in the fifth chapter.

3.3.5 Snowball Effects and Systemic Inertia

As it was presented, the various mechanisms are self-reinforcing and necessarily lead to the worsening of the situation. The more time is wasted, the higher the adverse effects. Sinn (2014, 2018) compares the public monetary flow to drug addiction or Dutch Disease.[33] Once individuals get used to a certain living standard, it is not politically feasible to deprive them of it. When the country's productivity does not cover such a living standard, it leads to high government deficits and further deterioration of the macroeconomic fundamentals (Sinn, 2018). Consequently, the countries gradually lose their national sovereignty and are increasingly dependent on centralised policymaking in the EU.

The presented section provided evidence that political integration cannot be successful without the proper alignment of macroeconomic fundamentals of all the member countries. The current mainstream ideology could produce major economic and political crises, which could lead to the collapse of the integration process. Alternatively, the policy-makers will '*conserve*' the situation, and the EU and the Euro Area countries will show significant economic stagnation in the next decades. Nevertheless, the possible stagnation cannot be maintained indefinitely and could ultimately lead to social unrest and other crises.

References

Afonso, A., Alves, J., & Balhote, R. (2019). Interactions between monetary and fiscal policies. *Journal of Applied Economics, 22*(1), 132–151. https://doi.org/10.1080/15140326.2019.1583309

Baumgarten, M., & Klodt, H. (2010). Greece and beyond: The debt mechanics of the Euro. *Aussenwirtschaft, 65*(4), 365–377. http://ux-tauri.unisg.ch/RePEc/usg/auswrt/AW_65-0403_Baumgarten-Klodt.pdf

Berend, I. T. (2017). *The contemporary crisis of the European Union: Prospects for the future*. Routledge. ISBN: 978-1138244191.

Broz, T. (2005). The theory of optimum currency areas: A literature review. *Privredna kretanja i ekonomska politika, 15*(104), 52–78. https://hrcak.srce.hr/18402

Cheung, Y.-W., Steinkamp, S., & Westermann, F. (2020). Capital flight to Germany: Two alternative measures. *Journal of International Money and Finance, 102*, 1–21. https://doi.org/10.1016/j.jimonfin.2019.102095

Coccia, M. (2018). *Does European Monetary Union increase government debt/GDP of countries? Preliminary statistical evidence* (CocciaLab Working Paper No. 34). National Research Council of Italy. Retrieved July 5, 2022, from https://papers.ssrn.com/sol3/papers.cfm?abstract_id=3188130

[33]The '*disease*' occurred in the 1960s when the Netherlands found a massive natural gas field in their territory. The sales of gas ultimately undermined the competitiveness of other economic sectors due to a wage contagion.

European Central Bank (ECB). (2016). *TARGET balances and the asset purchase programme* (Economic Bulletin No. 7/2016). Retrieved July 9, 2022, from https://www.ecb.europa.eu/pub/economic-bulletin/html/eb201607.en.html

European Commission. (2022a). *Financial assistance in the EU*. Retrieved August 5, 2022, from https://ec.europa.eu/info/business-economy-euro/economic-and-fiscal-policy-coordination/financial-assistance-eu/

European Commission. (2022b). *RRF: Update of the maximum financial contribution*. Retrieved August 12, 2022, from https://ec.europa.eu/info/sites/default/files/2022_06_30_update_maximum_financial_contribution_rrf_grants.pdf

Eurostat. (2022). *Eurostat database*. Retrieved September 21, 2022, from https://ec.europa.eu/eurostat

Feldstein, M. (2012). The failure of the Euro: The little currency that couldn't. *Foreign Affairs, 91*(1), 105–116. http://www.jstor.org/stable/23217153

Frankel, J. A., & Rose, A. K. (1998). The endogeneity of the optimum currency area criteria. *The Economic Journal, 108*(449), 1009–1025. http://www.jstor.org/stable/2565665

Friedman, M. (1997). Greece debt crisis: Milton Friedman's 1997 prediction of the Eurozone disaster. *The Australian Financial Review.*. https://www.afr.com/policy/greece-debt-crisis-milton-friedmans-1997-prediction-of-the-eurozone-disaster-20150706-gi5tgk

Institute of Empirical Economic Research. (2022). *Euro Crisis monitor dataset*. Retrieved August 12, 2022, from http://www.eurocrisismonitor.com/

Jager, J., & Hafner, K. A. (2013). The optimum currency area theory and the EMU. *Intereconomics, 48*(5), 315–322. https://doi.org/10.1007/s10272-013-0474-7

Jimoh, A. (2004). The monetary approach to exchange rate determination. *Journal of Economic Cooperation, 25*(2), 109–130. https://www.sesric.org/files/article/109.pdf

Kenen, P. (1969). The theory of optimum currency areas: An eclectic view. *Monetary Problems of the International Economy, 45*(3), 41–60.

Kunroo, M. H. (2015). Theory of optimum currency areas. *Review of Market Integration, 7*(2), 87–116. https://doi.org/10.1177/0974929216631381

Loužek, M. (2015). Eurozone crisis. *Prague Economic Papers, 24*(1), 88–104. https://doi.org/10.18267/j.pep.502

McKinnon, R. I. (1963). Optimum currency areas. *The American Economic Review, 53*(4), 717–725. http://www.jstor.org/stable/1811021

Minenna, M., Dosi, G., & Roventini, A. (2018). ECB monetary expansions and Euro Area TARGET2 imbalances: A balance-of-payment-based decomposition. *European Journal of Economics and Economic Policies: Intervention, 15*(2), 147–159. https://doi.org/10.4337/ejeep.2018.0038

Mody, A. (2018). *Eurotragedy: A drama in nine acts*. Oxford University Press. ISBN: 978-01-99-35138-1.

Monteverdi, A. (2016). *Optimum currency area theory and EMU: Lessons from the Euro crisis* (CROIE Working Paper No. 2/2016). CROIE. Retrieved July 11, 2022, from http://croie.luiss.it/files/2016/05/Monteverdi-OCA-and-EMU-rev-1.pdf

Mundell, R. A. (1961). A theory of optimum currency areas. *The American Economic Review, 51*(4), 657–665. http://www.jstor.org/stable/1812792

Reinhart, C. M., & Rogoff, K. S. (2013). *Financial and sovereign debt crises: Some lessons learned and those forgotten* (IMF Working Paper No. 13/266). International Monetary Fund. Retrieved July 9, 2022, from https://www.imf.org/external/pubs/ft/wp/2013/wp13266.pdf

Sinn, H.-W. (2012). *The European balance of payments crisis. CESifo Forum, 13*(1) https://www.ifo.de/DocDL/Forum-Sonderheft-Jan-2012.pdf

Sinn, H.-W. (2014). *The Euro trap: On bursting bubbles, budgets, and beliefs*. Oxford University Press. ISBN: 978-01-98-79144-7.

Sinn, H.-W. (2018). Brexit and the Euro crisis: What kind of union do we want? *Politická ekonomie, 66*(1), 3–19. https://doi.org/10.18267/j.polek.1174

Stiglitz, J. (2016). *The Euro: How a common currency threatens the future of Europe*. W.W. Norton. ISBN: 978-03-93-25402-0.

Wyplosz, C. (2016). The six flaws of the Eurozone. *Economic Policy, 31*(87), 559–606. https://doi.org/10.1093/epolic/eiw008

Chapter 4
Sovereign Debt Channels in the Euro Area

A proper analysis of possible debt channels in the Euro Area is crucial for three main reasons. First, the previous chapter has demonstrated that the current Euro Area environment is highly unstable, and the validity of various analyses depends on the identification of debt channels which are existing within the monetary union. Unfortunately, no study tried to identify the debt channels systemically. Second, austerity policy measures are often heavily criticised due to their poor results (for instance, see Prisecaru, 2013). In the case of high debt accumulation inertia, fiscal regulation and austerity measures are inefficient, the countries are bound to be less competitive, and the welfare of the citizens is lower. Finally, the analysis is fundamental in a historically low-inflationary (or even deflationary) environment where the effects of debt accumulation are not limited.[1]

Arguably, there is no finite debt accumulation horizon in the Euro Area. Thus, austerity measures are inefficient if they are not combined with structural changes in the Euro Area. The supranational powers of the EU should be reconsidered, and the structure of the Euro Area should be changed. It is evident that the situation cannot be solved politically to make the debt environment efficient and sustainable in the long term. The debt-accumulation mechanisms in the Euro Area are making the situation progressively worse over time.

The present chapter contains eight key mechanisms of debt accumulation in the Euro Area. I propose distinguishing between debt mechanisms that are working under the condition of full information, under information asymmetry, or the combination of both factors. The focus of this chapter on institutional features should help find an optimal policy and institutional mix, which would support the efficiency of the fiscal measures. Furthermore, the findings may help further clarify the problem

[1] The COVID-19 pandemic and the related worldwide crisis have lessened the weight of this argument recently. Nevertheless, the Euro Area showed low inflationary pressures from a historical point of view.

M. Bednář, *Fiscal Policy in the Southern European Union Countries*, Contributions to Finance and Accounting, https://doi.org/10.1007/978-3-031-29761-8_4

of whether there is a finite horizon of debt accumulation in the Euro Area. Each section of this chapter contains one debt channel and the related discussion.

4.1 Debt-Related Institutional Characteristics of the Euro Area

The institutional flaws of the Euro Area were discussed in the previous chapter. However, the following text focuses on the most important characteristics or flaws regarding debt accumulation. Policymakers and analysts need to recognise that the origin of debt crises is not always strictly fiscal. Fiscal austerity is a necessary but insufficient condition for preventing a debt crisis (Panizza, 2013). Masuch et al. (2017) claim that the quality of institutions is an important determinant of long-term growth in European countries. Moreover, the authors mention that sound institutions can mitigate the negative impacts of high indebtedness. The institutional design of the Euro Area plays a vital role in deficit tendencies and debt accumulation, significantly influencing the overall debt trend. According to Coccia (2018), statistical evidence shows that the dynamics of gross debt are significantly different between countries within and outside the Euro Area. Moreover, the results suggest that divergence is increasing.

The Euro Area suffers from a significant heterogeneity between the member countries, and this fact has many consequences. In short, one measure cannot fit all, which poses problems for both the functioning of the Euro Area and policy-making decisions. For instance, the ECB is not an independent entity because its national constituencies have different interests and do not share a common understanding of central banking (Wyplosz, 2016). Moreover, the fiscal regulations in the Euro Area are in direct conflict with the current situation and practices. On the one hand, the ECB's monetary policy is expansive, and the EU pursues policies of unemployment reduction and GDP growth.

On the other hand, the EU's constitutional balanced-budget amendments, the Stability and Growth Pact, and the so-called Fiscal Compact aim for countries to keep their budget deficits and overall indebtedness in the appropriate range. The approach seems schizophrenic at first sight, but it is a result of compromises within a highly heterogeneous entity.[2]

The Euro Area does not form an optimum currency area.[3] The countries' economies are not resilient against asymmetric shocks, which was revealed during the financial crisis of 2008–2009 and led to the sovereign debt crisis in the Euro Area. Another direct consequence of this mechanism is that the system requires constant

[2] Another direct consequence of the fact is that the fiscal rules are, historically, not taken very seriously.

[3] The well-known issue is also explained, for example, by Jager and Hafner (2013).

interventions,[4] making it unsustainable in this regard. Moreover, the recovery mechanisms of many economies are significantly weakened. Notably, this is the case in the EU4 countries where the common currency is unsuitable.[5] The fact further escalates the institutional and political problems.

Another critical institutional characteristic of the Euro Area is the socialisation of risks.[6] The same notion applies to rescue mechanisms. Without costs being fully internalised, there will always be motivations for some countries not to run sustainable fiscal policies and adhere to debt accumulation. The issue is the so-called Common Pool Problem, where agents do not fully internalise the tax burden of spending decisions (Alesina & Passalacqua, 2016). Some researchers, for example, Claeys (2017), propose that Europe should ultimately pursue the US model of federalism. However, even if this were done, the result would be unsustainable as some parts of Europe would permanently finance others. It is a demonstration of the fact that political unification cannot be forced without economic and social ties between the regions. All in all, the institutional design and the composition of the current Euro Area are forming the possibly strongest channel of debt accumulation.

4.2 Nature of Democracy and Political Cycles

According to Posner (2015), some researchers claim that democracies are bound to debt hoarding. When government policies have a significant distributional impact, various interest groups attempt to influence the outcome in line with their aims. Smaller and more coordinated interest groups are often more powerful than the majority. More specifically, there is a case when a stabilisation may also have significant impacts, especially in the Euro Area. Various groups may try to shift the burden of stabilisation onto other groups; the process is called the 'War of Attrition'. As a result, the groups may try to wait for the others out, prolonging the period without stabilisation (Alesina & Drazen, 1991). Arguably, these groups may consist of the financial sector and large companies that face prospects of falling demand. The theory cannot explain how deficit or debt reduction arises; however, it describes how the solution is postponed. A possibly balancing democratic mechanism is represented by influential leaders who can push uncomfortable policies

---

[4]The creation of offset mechanisms, such as forming a fiscal union in the Euro Area, would not solve the core of the problem. Direct interventions would still be necessary. Nevertheless, the option is not politically achievable.

[5]The real exchange rate is '*too strong*' for the countries, rendering them less competitive due to their comparatively weaker economic fundamentals, for example, relatively high unit labour costs compared to the respective profits or value-added. Nevertheless, some countries (for example, Germany or the Netherlands) benefit from the common currency per se due to their comparatively higher competitiveness and economic level.

[6]This factor would not be a problem if the Euro Area consisted of a relatively homogeneous group of countries.

(Posner, 2015). Nevertheless, the current Euro Area's leaders could not make such a change. The characteristics of democracy and the competition between interest groups in the Euro Area may provide another significant channel of debt accumulation.

Political cycles may also influence the debt situation. Debt may be used as a strategic variable. For instance, if the current government is not sure of its reappointment, it may want to choose to run budget deficits to influence the fiscal choices of future governments (Alesina & Tabellini, 1990). In addition, the debt is being snowballed as the next government may want to use the expenses to make the economy perform the same or even better than the previous government. Finally, the so-called political budget cycles consider the role of government deficits (and possible debts) before elections as a tool for the representatives to be re-elected. Yet, this proposition may explain only a relatively small departure from optimal policy. It cannot explain the long-lasting trend of debt accumulation (Alesina & Passalacqua, 2016).

4.3 Information Asymmetries

Many economic decisions would not be made with complete information; this fact also applies to the emergence of high government debts. The transmission mechanisms in the political market are arguably slower and less flexible. However, the outcomes are always demonstrated by the elections. It will always be easier to maintain the current status quo by claiming that we live in prosperous times and that a significant change could be harmful. This fallacy, directly connected to the effect of fiscal illusion, represents the argumentum ad antiquitatem (appeal to tradition). It completely ignores how a situation has evolved and neglects proper analysis of the problem.

The issue is very apparent in the Euro Area. Most politicians completely ignore the relevant structural problems of the monetary union. The strategy of the current president of the European Commission Ursula von der Leyen follows the principle. The strategy follows the so-called green deals, equalitarian and gender-oriented movements, and other agendas that are currently very popular (see Leyen, 2019). These topics should not be the priorities[7] when considering the most critical institutional flaws of the EU and the Euro Area. Nevertheless, it can be argued that Leyen's strategy is well thought out, and its ultimate purpose is not to serve the people of the EU, which is a valid argument. Politicians have individual motivations to act accordingly to the political cycle. The fallacy is problematic and, arguably, was escalated by the 'Keynesian' policy stand over time. The information asymmetry can affect both politicians and voters.

[7] Arguably, some parts of these arrangements should not be pursued at all.

4.4 Keynesian Stabilisation Efforts

The Keynesian practice aims to smooth the economic cycle with the argument that it promotes economic efficiency. Notably, during periods of recession, higher government spending or lower taxes may help economic recovery. However, the idea is accompanied by many issues. First, it poses characteristics of central planning the economy, which is intrinsically problematic, and, in reality, hardly achievable. This is due to many factors; for example, to interpret the economic data correctly, consider the issue of time lags, the efficiency of such policies, and other factors. Second, structural factors are often misinterpreted in economic practice. Structural factors are those that are not connected to the Keynesian idea of sub-optimal demand. Paradoxically, such characteristics are taken as support for the central idea of fiscal stimulus. It is very apparent in the current Euro Area as its structural and institutional faults are often overlooked. Third, the argument of stabilisation lacks seriousness when the policies continue to be highly expansive even in 'better times' of higher economic growth.

The Keynesian approach is connected to many issues arising from political motivations. This is the problem of misuse, as the policies should be countercyclical, and the debt-to-GDP ratio should not follow an upward trend (Alesina & Passalacqua, 2016). Politicians are eager to implement Keynesian stimulus in recessions. However, they do not counter-balance it in times of expansion by creating budget surpluses. In this case, some theoretical explanations were also used to support the fact of rising government debt. For instance, Barro's tax smoothing hypothesis implies a distribution of tax burden across generations (see Barro, 1979).[8] Nevertheless, the proposition of government as a strictly rational central planner pursuing overall welfare seems not plausible because of the above reasons. In addition, the motivations in the current Euro Area follow a different objective of preserving the current status quo by using '*all that it takes*'.[9]

4.5 Reputation and Expectations

A good reputation of an entity helps to maintain large amounts of sovereign debt by inducing a better reaction from lending subjects (Cole & Kehoe, 1998). The same concept concerns groups of countries (or a monetary union) as well. However, in the case of major structural problems in the Euro Area, the reputation is diminishing,

[8]Even though the basis of this idea is strictly non-Keynesian.

[9]This is a reference to the famous 2012 statement of Mario Draghi (former president of the ECB), who declared: '*We will do whatever it takes to save the euro*'. It also serves as a reference to the arguably misleading 2010 statement of the current ECB's president Christine Lagarde (IMF's managing director at that time): '*We violated all the rules because we wanted to close ranks and really rescue the eurozone*'.

progressively putting more pressure on the most indebted countries. It can be argued that the debt structure is changing over time, as more debt is now 'internal or common EU debt'. Nevertheless, it does not support the standard definition of internal debt because the Euro Area is not a single country but an entity made of different countries.

Lenders' expectations about the politico-financial outcome are self-fulfilling and can increase the likelihood of financial and political crises (Vaugirard, 2005). As a result, they may be willing to lend less and require higher interest rates. The former is mitigated by the current monetary policies, keeping the interest rates low. However, negative expectations of the public could weaken aggregate demand, putting even more pressure on public stimulus—rising indebtedness. These two channels represent another debt channel, worsening the situation.

4.6 Strict Preferences

Arguably, a particular debt level is the consequence of long-term national preferences. The argument is compelling and is possibly one of the debt channels. A simple explanation is that people are willing to be better off in the short term at the expense of long-run problems because their life is finite, and they have a strong short-time preference. Additionally, the motivation is strengthened in the Euro Area due to the socialisation of risks. This may be the case of Greece, which received significant external help during the financial crisis of 2008–2009.

Fochmann et al. (2014) conducted a behavioural experiment and found that the main behavioural force behind public debt is an intergenerational transmission of the tax burden. Even though a massive portion of the accumulated debt in the experiment was explicitly connected to serious risks of a financial meltdown, followed by penalty taxation, the individuals did not vote for a debt reduction. It was also the case of small groups with strong social ties. The authors concluded that they observed much less sense of intergenerational fairness or altruistic concerns than expected. As long as it is in individuals' selfish interest, they do not hesitate to shift the heavy burden of public debt to the next generation. Without the transmission possibility, the individuals voted for a prudent debt policy and wanted to avoid excessive indebtedness by all means (ibid.). The observation follows the debt trend of many developed economies and puts into question the standard economic rationale.

4.7 Current Macroeconomic Conditions and COVID-19 Pandemic

Most Euro Area countries have already accumulated a substantial portion of real debts, which is challenging to maintain through debt service repayments, and even more challenging lower. The sovereign debt crisis from 2008 to 2009 has not been solved.[10] In early 2020, European countries were significantly hit by the COVID-19 crisis. As a result, the debt ratios drastically increased, as was the case during the previous financial crisis. The issue is linked to the non-optimality of the currency area; another significant asymmetric shock triggered the same mechanism and consequences seen from 2008 to 2009—the vicious circle of dampened economic growth and overall competitiveness. Furthermore, high initial indebtedness, along with the institutional dysfunctionality of the Euro Area, creates a stronger demand for a more politically controlled union and more expansive economic policies (Bordo & James, 2008).

4.8 Future Prospects and Other Factors

The future may bring both unexpected and expected economic shocks. In February of 2022, the Russian invasion of Ukraine put pressure on European consumer and investor sentiment, along with increased social expenditure,[11] military expenditure, and global safety concerns. Moreover, prices of selected commodities such as energy and food items sharply increased. Ergo, the economies (along with their debt levels) were hit by another significant shock not long after the lockdowns associated with the government responses to the COVID-19 pandemic.

While the unexpected events cannot be predicted, there is already indisputable evidence of another factor that will consistently put more and more pressure on government finance. The aspect is population ageing.[12] The phenomenon has various channels of influence over the indebtedness of the countries. First, it encourages more public spending on social benefits and pensions as the population ages. Second, there is evidence that older people prefer increasing government debt to increasing tax rates. The problem was theoretically evaluated by Brennan (2012) and empirically validated by Fochmann et al. (2014).

In addition, another geopolitical occurrence is the ever-increasing competition between the 'old Western advanced democracies' (the group of countries including the EU and the Euro Area) and the rising superpowers such as China. It represents

[10]Some analysts, politicians, and the public did not pay enough attention to the issue because of relatively strong economic growth after 2012, which was associated with cyclical over-optimism.

[11]Expenditure associated with the integration of migrants. For instance, refer to Zubíková (2019).

[12]See, for example, Auerbach (2016) for a more detailed discussion.

another significant debt incentive as the countries try to improve their positions or slow down the loss in general competitiveness.

References

Alesina, A., & Drazen, A. (1991). Why are stabilizations delayed? *The American Economic Review, 81*(5), 1170–1188. https://search.proquest.com/docview/233042425

Alesina, A., & Passalacqua, A. (2016). The political economy of government debt. In *Handbook of macroeconomics* (pp. 2599–2651). Elsevier. https://doi.org/10.1016/bs.hesmac.2016.03.014

Alesina, A., & Tabellini, G. (1990). A positive theory of fiscal deficits and government debt. *The Review of Economic Studies, 57*(3), 403–414. https://doi.org/10.2307/2298021

Auerbach, A. J. (2016). Long-term fiscal sustainability in advanced economies. *Asia & the Pacific Policy Studies, 3*(2), 142–154. https://doi.org/10.1002/app5.131

Barro, R. J. (1979). On the determination of the public debt. *Journal of Political Economy, 87*(5, Part 1), 940–971. https://doi.org/10.1086/260807

Bordo, M., & James, H. (2008). *A long term perspective on the Euro* (Economic Paper No. 307). European Commission. Retrieved July 7, 2022, from https://ec.europa.eu/economy_finance/publications/pages/publication12121_en.pdf

Brennan, G. (2012). The political economy of public debt. *Constitutional Political Economy, 23*(3), 182–198. https://doi.org/10.1007/s10602-012-9124-5

Claeys, G. (2017). *The missing pieces of the Euro architecture* (Bruegel Policy Contribution Issue No. 28). Bruegel. Retrieved July 5, 2022, from http://bruegel.org/wp-content/uploads/2017/10/PC-28-2017.pdf

Coccia, M. (2018). *Does European Monetary Union increase government debt/GDP of countries? Preliminary statistical evidence* (CocciaLab Working Paper No. 34). National Research Council of Italy. Retrieved July 5, 2022, from https://papers.ssrn.com/sol3/papers.cfm?abstract_id=3188130

Cole, H. L., & Kehoe, P. J. (1998). Models of sovereign debt: Partial versus general reputations. *International Economic Review, 39*(1), 55–70. https://doi.org/10.2307/2527230

Fochmann, M., Sadrieh, A., & Weimann, J. (2014). Understanding the emergence of public debt. *SSRN Electronic Journal.* https://doi.org/10.2139/ssrn.2436292

Jager, J., & Hafner, K. A. (2013). The optimum currency area theory and the EMU. *Intereconomics, 48*(5), 315–322. https://doi.org/10.1007/s10272-013-0474-7

Leyen, U. v. d. (2019). *A union that strives for more* (Political Guidelines for the Next European Commission 2019-2024). Retrieved July 6, 2022, from https://ec.europa.eu/commission/sites/beta-political/files/political-guidelines-next-commission_en.pdf

Masuch, K., Moshammer, E., & Pierluigi, B. (2017). Institutions, public debt and growth in Europe. *Public Sector Economics, 41*(2), 159–205. https://doi.org/10.3326/pse.41.2.2

Panizza, U. (2013). The origins and resolution of debt crises: It is not always fiscal! *Comparative Economic Studies, 55*(3), 431–453. https://doi.org/10.1057/ces.2013.18

Posner, P. L. (2015). The politics of fiscal austerity: Democracies and foresight. *Indiana Journal of Global Legal Studies, 22*(2), 433–485. https://doi.org/10.2979/indjglolegstu.22.2.433

Prisecaru, P. (2013). Austerity versus Stimulating the Growth in EU. *Knowledge Horizons — Economics, 5*(3), 61–65. https://ideas.repec.org/a/khe/journl/v5y2013i3p61-65.html

Vaugirard, V. (2005). Crony capitalism and sovereign default. *Open Economies Review, 16*(1), 77–99. https://doi.org/10.1007/s11079-005-5333-0

Wyplosz, C. (2016). The six flaws of the Eurozone. *Economic Policy, 31*(87), 559–606. https://doi.org/10.1093/epolic/eiw008

Zubíková, A. (2019). *Integration of immigrants in the EU_15: Success or failure?* (pp. 367–384). Proceedings of the 12th Economics & Finance Conference, Dubrovnik. International Institute of

Social and Economic Sciences (IISES). https://www.iises.net/proceedings/12th-economics-finance-conference-dubrovnik/table-of-content/detail?article=integration-of-immigrants-in-the-eu-15-success-or-failure-

Chapter 5
European Fiscal and Debt Union

Immediately after experiencing the worst effects of the previous financial crisis of 2008–2009, many economists shared the idea that the Euro Area can only survive if it is complemented by a fiscal union (Fuest & Peichl, 2012). In particular, some analysts claim that the financial crisis has shown that the Euro Area needs to be complemented with a high degree of centralisation of fiscal transfers. Otherwise, the system is unsustainable (Bénassy-Quéré et al., 2016). Creating a fiscal union would help the Euro Area get closer to the optimal currency area because it could deal with asymmetric shocks and other issues that challenge the stability of the monetary union. The idea is being discussed up to this day. Therefore, the present chapter examines if a deeper fiscal integration would solve the issues of the Euro Area and, more importantly, if the centralised policy reaction to the COVID-19 pandemic in the form of debt redistribution was appropriate. Nevertheless, the text provides a rigorous macroeconomic analysis as it does not deal with normative political aspects.[1]

The chapter is designed to help the reader comprehend the topic in a structured manner. First, it defines what a fiscal union is. Second, it lists potential costs and benefits associated with the possible creation of a fiscal union within the Euro Area member countries. Third, it provides an overview and discussion about implicit assumptions needed for the fiscal union to work properly. Fourth, it analyses the issue of symmetric shocks, which is rarely examined. Finally, it analyses the situation and policy responses to the COVID-19 crisis and centralised debt creation.

[1]These include the potential political feasibility of centralised fiscal decision-making.

M. Bednář, *Fiscal Policy in the Southern European Union Countries*, Contributions to Finance and Accounting, https://doi.org/10.1007/978-3-031-29761-8_5

5.1 Definition of a Fiscal Union

A fiscal union or robust centralisation of fiscal transfers between some regions would represent another step in the European integration process. It needs two important aspects: a mechanism for pooling resources to provide for expenditure and governance of such a mechanism (Iara, 2016). In addition, a fiscal union in the case of the Euro Area may but does not have to include several elements: fiscal rules, policy coordination and supervision, a crisis resolution mechanism, joint guarantee for government debt, fiscal equalisation with other mechanisms for transfers between countries, and a larger common budget and European taxes (Fuest & Peichl, 2012). A fiscal union can be achieved in many ways, for example, by creating a single finance ministry and finance minister or even by emissions of euro-bonds (Hallett, 2017). It should be noted that the current integration architecture of the Euro Area (or even the EU) already contains some elements of a fiscal union: the common budget, supra-national regulatory rules, the EU's own revenue sources, harmonisation of indirect taxes, and relevant monitoring practices. Furthermore, we have seen a very sharp incline towards Eurobonds as a reaction to the COVID-19 crisis. In July 2020, the European Council agreed to issue European sovereign bonds of 750 billion EUR, branded as the so-called Next Generation EU package, which can be considered a complement to the common EU budget.

5.2 Potential Benefits and Costs

Allard et al. (2013), together with some economists, argue that a robust centralisation of fiscal transfers would decrease the likelihood of future crises, their magnitudes, and systemic spillovers. If one country experiences a severe depression while other countries would have the capacity to help, then they could simply shift their resources through fiscal transfers and solve the issue. Other benefits may include gains from better coordination of policies within the Euro Area (the system may be less prone to externalities arising from different policies) or increasing returns to scale. It may also help to strengthen the fiscal discipline[2] within the Area. Furthermore, some of the member countries may experience reputation gains. A fiscal union may also help to make the labour markets of the member countries more homogeneous through the centralisation of unemployment benefits and pension systems (Cottarelli, 2016).

Nevertheless, it has been both theoretically and empirically shown that robust centralisation suffers from the issue of asymmetric information, as mentioned by Hayek (1988). Therefore, the management of the system would be rather rigid. Other potential cons include political costs (disputes), social costs (regulatory changes),

---

[2]Note that this point is very disputable because it could promote moral hazard with the opposite effect. Refer to the text below.

Table 5.1 Potential benefits and costs of a fiscal union

Potential benefits	Potential costs
Better OCA[a] criteria alignment	Breach of national sovereignty (democratic deficit)
Improvement in fiscal discipline	The problem of moral hazard[b]
Coordination gains, economies of scale and scope	Centralisation of costs, information asymmetries
Correction mechanism for negative externalities	Possibility of stronger government failures
	Constant interventions within a faulty monetary union
	Political and social costs (disputes, social unrests)

Source: Own processing
[a]Optimum currency area; refer to the third chapter
[b]Moral hazard is a situation where an economic actor (specific member country) has the incentive to increase its exposure to risk because it does not bear the full costs of that risk. This led to excessive accumulation of debt by some countries in the past

and moral hazards (Allard et al., 2013). There would be no guarantee that a fiscal union would strengthen the overall financial discipline. Moreover, history shows that citizens will not accept taxation without representation. The union would suffer from a democratic deficit, an issue for the whole EU.[3] It could lead to even worse government failures than those that can be currently observed on the national level. In addition, introducing new taxes could lead to a higher financial and bureaucratic burden. The snowball effect, which is already in place in the case of many EU institutions, could be even more substantial. Paradoxically, further instability in the Euro Area could occur.

Some analysts also overlook the fundamental problem of fiscal policy as it suffers from various time lags. The statistical delay could be mitigated under the assumption that the member countries share a high degree of homogeneity in macroeconomic imbalances (Alessandrini & Fratianni, 2016). However, this assumption is not fulfilled. Other delays include a lag in recognition of a problem, decision lag, legislative implementation issues, and a delay when policymakers can observe the desired effects of a specific policy. Not surprisingly, aggregate demand shifts are complicated to manage in practice properly. Finally, the concept of a fiscal union is problematic when a monetary union has systematic flaws and is prone to recurring instabilities.[4] The overview of benefits and costs is provided in Table 5.1.

According to the analysis, the idea that the current Euro Area can be 'repaired' through creating a fiscal union is unlikely to be correct. The costs presumably

[3]The officials claimed that they were trying to make the decision-making '*more efficient*'. The argument was made by EU officials when adjusting the voting system and voting weights after the 2009 Lisbon Treaty. However, the efficiency gains are at the expense of the sovereignty of smaller countries.

[4]The issue was discussed in the previous chapters.

outweigh the potential benefits of the centralised fiscal transfer system. Furthermore, some of the claimed benefits would possibly be non-existent.

5.3 Implicit Assumptions of a Viable Fiscal Centralisation

The path to a working monetary union by establishing robust centralisation of fiscal transfers lies on many implicit assumptions that are rarely discussed. According to my research, the assumptions are as follows:

1. Similar initial situation (homogeneity) of the member countries
2. An appropriate size of the common budget
3. Satisfactory efficiency of fiscal transfers, which could compensate for lower labour, price, and wage flexibility
4. High efficiency of fiscal regulations when determining rights and obligations
   - Compliance with the no-bailout clause in the fiscal policy decisions
   - Sustainability of the common budget
   - Independence between fiscal revenues and expenditures
5. Ability to manage a high degree of centralisation
6. Democratic principles of the policy
7. Precise and duly noted information
8. Appropriate quality of fiscal governance and learning from past mistakes
   - Stabilisation effects of the common fiscal policy
   - No negative spillovers of the common fiscal policy

First, the common budget of the EU and the relevant fiscal transfers would have to be significantly larger than in history. It could mean that the sufficient values of budget revenues and expenditures could reach tens of GDP percentage points. For instance, fiscal transfers in the USA are enormous (see Dreyer & Schmid, 2015). Whether it would be possible to gather so many resources or not is an open question.

Another assumption concerns the high efficiency of fiscal policy, which would require fiscal multipliers to be quite high across the Euro Area. There is a large body of evidence (see Hagen, 2014) that has concluded that the response of fiscal transfers to instabilities in the existing federations is rather weak. In the USA, such transfers offset approximately 10% of asymmetric shocks between the countries. In the case of Germany, the number is even lower (ibid.). If the multipliers were not high enough, the EU common budget would have to expand even more.[5] In addition, Vranceanu and Besancenot (2013) showed that multipliers are negatively affected by the amount of public debt, especially when the ratio of public debt to GDP exceeds 150%, which was relevant for Greece and Italy at the end of 2021. We may expect

[5] I provide evidence that the multipliers were prohibitively low before the financial crisis in the eighth chapter.

these ratios to rise for more countries over time due to the COVID-19 crisis and other factors such as those related to the Russian invasion of Ukraine in 2022.

The more significant the common budget, the more problems it could create. In principle, higher-income earners should oppose the fiscal union, while low-income earners should support it because of the redistribution. However, these views among member countries are distorted due to their political leaders. Left-wing political parties tend to be more inclined to support the creation of the fiscal union because of comparatively higher benefits for low-income, underemployed, and unemployed individuals (Franchino & Segatti, 2019).

Additionally, the more the decision is centralised and the farther the decision-making from individuals or member countries, the less accountable it is, and the higher the potential democratic deficit is. According to Iara (2016), GNI-type contributions would be most suitable to get the appropriate budget revenues, which would also mean that the connection between tax collection and specific fiscal policy would be very loose. It would possibly create political disputes among the countries.

Furthermore, a fiscal union can be seen as a way of sharing risks. However, it only works under the assumption of non-existent moral hazard. The creation of fiscal unions would practically (and again) break the no-bailout rule as it is evident that the policymakers would use it for such a purpose. The situation could be compared to the one before the financial crisis of 2008–2009 when there was a uniform market interest rate for all of the Euro Area, and the countries with usually higher interest rates exploited the situation for their short-term benefit. It should be mentioned that the price of freedom and prosperity is individual risk and responsibility.

The main purpose of fiscal unions should not be risk-sharing (Hagen, 2014). Instead, they should promote fiscal responsibility and the sustainability of public finances through their system of responsibilities and assignments. However, I am unaware of evidence that a fiscal union would promote sustainability. Politicians usually make short-term decisions due to the political cycle. For instance, the solutions to the previous financial crisis were of such nature and did not lead to any significant progress. Politicians are often not willing to learn from past mistakes. In addition, the common monetary policy in the Euro Area shares these aspects, even though it should be independent of politics.

Furthermore, the quality of fiscal governance could be lower because politicians would have stronger motivations (profits) to pursue their self-interest.[6] At the same time, the relevant budget constraint would be weaker as the decisions would be less accountable because of the distance from the affected regions. Some argue that the current EU budget is made sustainable by law; however, this evidence is insignificant as it historically accounted only for approximately 1% of the EU's GNI. Overall, no economist should argue that this form of governance would definitely exhibit returns to scale.

[6] Similarly, particular interest groups are more influential on the supra-national level as the incentives are also more pronounced.

Moreover, it has been both theoretically and empirically proved that massive centralisation is impossible to manage. Countries such as the Czech Republic, Poland, Slovakia, Hungary, and others experienced the dysfunctionality of communism[7] first-hand. Moreover, fiscal policy tends to exhibit adverse spillovers as it may influence other countries apart from the target region. The situation is even more complicated when considering the differences in the basic socio-economic variables of the Euro Area member countries. Drea (2016) mentions that '*retrofitting*' a higher level of political and fiscal integration to a monetary union already in place will be very difficult. The situation is problematic due to public antipathy towards greater integration, notable differences in current debt levels, relatively low economic growth, and high youth unemployment in some EU member countries—most notably in the EU4 countries.

Furthermore, there is evidence that the European fiscal rules have become overcomplicated, inefficient, and open to widespread manipulation (Drea, 2016). The EU decision-makers failed in this area as the Euro Area countries must deal with an increasingly complex set of fiscal rules[8] and their inconsistent implementation. These rules break national sovereignty, deny the functionality of automatic stabilisers, act as a pro-cyclical policy in recessions, and do not incorporate future trends such as population ageing.

Woźniakowski (2017) mentions how problematic the Euro Area's current state is. The member countries cannot use independent exchange rates to deal with the shocks. However, they also cannot flexibly use the fiscal policy as they are constrained by the EU's rules for national fiscal policies. Finally, common fiscal governance arguably cannot replace the need for production factors, price, and wage flexibility when considering all of the arguments.

Evidently, seeking the creation of a fiscal union is not a viable answer to the structural problems of the Euro Area. The EU should maintain national fiscal autonomy and simplify its budgetary rules (Drea, 2016). Logically, the countries that do not sufficiently fulfil the OCA criteria are left with only fiscal policy to stabilise their national economies; the policy needs to be kept decentralised. In addition, the causes of the economic crisis were national.[9] Therefore, the solutions should also be national (Cózar, 2017).

I conclude that there is no single assumption that would not be seriously challenged. In fact, many of them would not be fulfilled.

[7] It was socialism in practice, to be precise.

[8] Such as the Fiscal Stability Treaty or other rules that are trying to correct various imbalances within the region.

[9] I am referring to the individual structural differences in the EU and the Euro Area, such as the health of a country's financial system.

5.4 Economic Shocks and Centralised Fiscal Policy

The very design of the Euro Area is producing asymmetric shocks, which is an issue that is rarely analysed. The fiscal union discussion is about making the Euro Area more stable. Nevertheless, the idea neglects the development of potential products and other main variables in periods of relative stability. Analysts are afraid of asymmetric shocks, according to the OCA theory. However, economists usually do not mention how these asymmetric shocks occur. Consider the example of the financial crisis, which started the European public debt crisis and led to discussions about creating a fiscal union. It is evident that the initial shock (lower demand, higher unemployment, or a challenge for public finance, among other factors) was mostly symmetric as it hit all the Euro Area countries. Nevertheless, it later produced asymmetric responses among the member countries. Analysis of symmetric shocks bears the same or even higher importance when the monetary union is not functioning properly.

The conclusion is that a focus on the very design and structure of the monetary union is needed when assessing the feasibility of establishing mechanisms for centralised fiscal transfers. This way, it would be possible to deal with some of the asymmetric shocks and promote competitiveness at the same time. Arguably, there is no emphasis on competitive advantages. A higher degree of integration—a 'stronger union' does not necessarily mean higher competitiveness. Arguably, the design of the monetary union should be as transparent as possible, which means that the less the need to regulate it, the better it is. The more interventions, the higher the risk of failure and the more significant the implicit assumptions of a viable fiscal centralisation.

A 'strong' euro has been a concern for many analysts and policymakers. A strong exchange rate contributes to low inflation and GDP growth rates, making the reduction of public and private debt more painful and prolonged (Belke & Volz, 2015). In the past, it helped the inflation rate to get lower through its effect on import prices, which was an issue for the ECB and its target. Furthermore, countries suffering lack of competitiveness were not able to adequately or swiftly recover from the recession. Therefore, these exporters are not in a good position and GDP growth has been dampened (ibid.). Stronger euro undoubtedly worsens the competitiveness of some members, especially the EU4 countries. Exporters from the EU4 currently find themselves in a tight spot as their exports are more expensive due to the strong currency.

Moreover, the symmetric shocks produced by the uniform exchange rate affect the sectoral structure of the countries because export and import capabilities significantly differ across individual industries. In addition, the governments of the countries, which are negatively affected, may be encouraged to run expansionary policies. A common mechanism of fiscal transfers is unlikely to solve this problem.

According to Hagen (2014), it is wrong to think that a fiscal union would compensate for the loss of control over monetary policy at the national level. Such a mechanism would stabilise the individual economies around the average cyclical position of the monetary union. Technically, it does not necessarily mean that it would lead to more stable output and employment in the member countries. In addition, the potential benefits of a fiscal union would depend on the nature of the shocks, which makes the monetary union unstable. Moreover, as the situations of various member countries differ, the common fiscal policy would not be neutral and would have to be frequently used. Such characteristics tell that the system would not be sustainable. A devaluation per se is not a solution to the problem.

The macroeconomic imbalances of the Euro Area should be resolved primarily by structural adjustments. The EU should focus on competitiveness, not on how to 'tweak' and 'repair' the dysfunctional system. Establishing a fiscal union would represent a permanent redistribution mechanism from the Northern to the Southern countries. This would not necessarily mean the end of the euro currency. However, it would mean a fundamental change in the structure of the Euro Area, where only the well-performing economies with similar characteristics should belong. The solutions need to focus on the long term.

Furthermore, the endogeneity argument, which asserts that by reinforcing the integration process, the group of countries will become OCA, is shaky in its foundations and represents a utopian ideal. Policies should follow smaller steps when the final destination is uncertain.

Overall, the current Euro Area should focus on competitive advantages, long-term policies and transparent system design rather than trying to fix the system by establishing a fiscal union that would require constant government interventions.

5.5 COVID-19 Pandemic and European Debt Union

The COVID-19 crisis and related issues after 2020 led the European Union leaders to push forward various 'packages' in the form of a significant fiscal stimulus. Unfortunately, the funds are being borrowed. Hence, another discussion has emerged. The European Union and the Euro Area are becoming increasingly closer to what may be defined as a debt union. In principle, this would lead to a permanent sharing of public debts and the associated risks among the countries. As mentioned earlier, the EU4 countries may benefit from these actions in the short term. However, such a risk-sharing will inevitably lead to all the adverse effects that we have seen earlier, particularly during and after the financial crisis of 2008–2009. These include reinforced moral hazard, degradation of current account balances, loss of competitiveness, and other factors. Ultimately, the mix worsens macroeconomic efficiency, lowers potential GDPs, and destabilises the most vulnerable economies.

In short, debt sharing is a more extreme form of a supranational fiscal transfer system, which has played only a minor role so far.[10] The leaders are escalating their actions, and paradoxically, they are escalating the issues analysed in this chapter in

[10] When compared to national fiscal systems.

the long term. Based on the findings in this chapter, we can conclude that the attempt to construct a 'debt union' is a wrong policy choice that will affect all the EU countries negatively.

References

Allard, C., et al. (2013). *Toward a fiscal union for the Euro Area.* International Monetary Fund. ISBN: 978-14-8430-737-3.

Alessandrini, P., & Fratianni, M. (2016). In the absence of fiscal union, the Eurozone needs a more flexible monetary policy. *PSL Quarterly Review, 68*(275), 279–296. https://ojs.uniroma1.it/index.php/PSLQuarterlyReview/article/view/13231

Belke, A. H., & Volz, U. (2015). The strong Euro: Challenges for the European Central Bank and implications for the global economy. *AEI Insights, 1-2015*(1), 53–68. https://aei.um.edu.my/the-strong-euro-challenges-for-the-european-central-bank-and-implications-for-the-global-economy

Bénassy-Quéré, A., Ragot, X., & Wolff, G. B. (2016). *Which fiscal union for the Euro Area?* (Les notes du conseil d'analyse économique No. 29). French Council of Economic Analysis. Retrieved July 14, 2022, from http://www.cae-eco.fr/IMG/pdf/cae-note029-en.pdf

Cottarelli, C. (2016). A European fiscal union: The case for a larger central budget. *Economia Politica, 33*(1), 1–8. https://doi.org/10.1007/s40888-016-0026-2

Cózar, M. M. (2017). The only feasible fiscal union for the Euro Area. *European View, 16*(1), 23–32. https://doi.org/10.1007/s12290-017-0431-0

Drea, E. (2016). Nobody told me we could do this: Why fiscal union is not the answer to Eurozone woes. *European View, 15*(2), 315–324. https://doi.org/10.1007/s12290-016-0406-6

Dreyer, J. K., & Schmid, P. A. (2015). Fiscal federalism in monetary unions: Hypothetical fiscal transfers within the Euro-Zone. *International Review of Applied Economics, 29*(4), 506–532. https://doi.org/10.1080/02692171.2015.1016407

Fuest, C., & Peichl, A. (2012). *European fiscal union: What is it? Does it work? And are there really 'no alternatives'?* (IZA Policy Paper No. 39). Institute for the Study of Labor. Retrieved July 14, 2022, from http://ftp.iza.org/pp39.pdf

Franchino, F., & Segatti, P. (2019). Public opinion on the Eurozone fiscal union: Evidence from survey experiments in Italy. *Journal of European Public Policy, 26*(1), 126–148. https://doi.org/10.1080/13501763.2017.1400087

Hagen, J., & v. (2014). Governance of the Euro Area: fiscal union, debt union, fiscal freedom. *Wirtschaftsdienst, 94*(S1), 23–27. https://doi.org/10.1007/s10273-014-1646-1

Hallett, A. H. (2017). Fiscal autonomy vs. fiscal federalism in the Euro Zone. *Economia Politica, 34*(2), 179–188. https://doi.org/10.1007/s40888-017-0066-2

Hayek, F. A. v. (1988). *The fatal conceit: The errors of socialism.* Routledge. ISBN: 978-0415008204.

Iara, A. (2016). Revenue for EMU: A contribution to the debate on fiscal union. *CESifo Economic Studies, 62*(2), 301–331. https://doi.org/10.1093/cesifo/ifw012

Vranceanu, R., & Besancenot, D. (2013). The spending multiplier in a time of massive public debt: The Euro-Area case. *Applied Economics Letters, 20*(8), 758–762. https://doi.org/10.1080/13504851.2012.741674

Woźniakowski, T. P. (2017). Why the sovereign debt crisis could lead to a federal fiscal union: The paradoxical origins of fiscalization in the United States and insights for the European Union. *Journal of European Public Policy, 25*(4), 630–649. https://doi.org/10.1080/13501763.2017.1285340

Chapter 6
Specific Characteristics of EU4 Economies

As mentioned in the Introduction, four Southern EU countries were selected for the analysis. These include Italy, Spain, Portugal, and Greece—the EU4 countries. As a starting point of the analysis, it is crucial to evaluate these countries' overall macroeconomic position (both in absolute and relative terms). The reason is that fiscal indicators are strongly interconnected with the real economy. Therefore, the findings will help assess the countries' fiscal conditions and macroeconomic linkages in time and space.

The chapter has three parts from the point of view of used indicators. First, it examines the positions of the countries in the world and each other using basic macroeconomic variables and composite indices. The indices contain some qualitative measures, which are also desirable for the analysis. Second, it presents a summary of the developments in the economies by analysing the developments of key macroeconomic indicators, including their estimated natural (equilibrium) levels. Third, a cluster analysis is performed to obtain a representative estimate of the countries' positions.

6.1 Main Country Characteristics

Currently, the EU4 countries are considered to be democratic and relatively well-developed mixed[1] economies. Table 6.1 shows that Italy and Spain are by far the largest economies that are also important in the world. Hence, the economic instabilities of the two countries are much more pronounced in the EU and the Euro Area. The structural characteristics of the countries differ to some extent. However, the common sectors include agriculture, tourism, and shipping due to their favourable

[1]The designation '*market economies*' would be imprecise because of the existence of a significant amount of regulations in the economies.

M. Bednář, *Fiscal Policy in the Southern European Union Countries*, Contributions to Finance and Accounting, https://doi.org/10.1007/978-3-031-29761-8_6

Table 6.1 Selected macroeconomic indicators—EU4, 2021

	Total GDP (PPP, billions of international dollars)		GDP per capita (PPP, international dollars)	
Country	2021 value	World position	2021 value	World position
Italy	2734	15/193	46,161	32/191
Spain	1983	19/193	41,839	41/191
Portugal	380	55/193	36,844	45/191
Greece	344	58/193	32,218	54/191
EU19 average	921	35/193	54,647	22/191
EU27 average	804	39/193	50,834	37/191
World average	757	–	23,118	–

	General unemployment rate		General government gross debt	
Country	2021 value	World position	2021 value	World position
Italy	9.5%	77/107	150.9%	184/190
Spain	14.8%	96/107	118.7%	174/190
Portugal	6.6%	50/107	127.5%	178/190
Greece	15.0%	97/107	198.9%	188/190
EU19 average	7.2%	57/107	83.0%	146/190
EU27 average	6.7%	54/107	73.4%	130/190
World average	8.5%	–	66.5%	–

Note: Simple arithmetic averages are used. Other indicators, such as inflation and current account balances, are not shown due to their complicated interpretability of world standings
Source: IMF (2022), own calculations and processing

geographical location (see Eurostat, 2022). According to the GDP per capita measure, which approximates living standards, Italy and Spain are also the most developed economies. Nevertheless, Portugal and Greece are not positioned significantly behind.

Furthermore, the general unemployment rate and general government gross debt disclose some of the most problematic issues in the EU4 countries. Italy, Spain, and Greece suffer from prohibitively high unemployment rates, even in the world context. Concurrently, all four countries exhibit considerably high levels of indebtedness. It is important to mention that the latter two variables are both causes and consequences of their macroeconomic imbalances.

The EU4 countries went through their 'golden ages' in history. For Italy and Greece, it was the period of Ancient Rome and Ancient Greece. Meanwhile, for Spain and Portugal, it was the European colonial era. The countries experienced dynamic development during the twentieth century, in line with the development in Europe. In 1999, three of the countries joined the Euro Area and adopted the common currency. Greece adopted the common euro currency 2 years later, in 2001, and was suspected of reporting falsified government accounts afterwards (see OECD, 2005). Joining the Euro Area was arguably one of the roots of the ongoing European debt crisis.[2] The financial crisis of 2008–2009, which began to show its negative effects in the second quarter of 2008 in the EU, has uncovered deep inefficiencies in the economies. In general, the EU4 countries suffer from structural flaws in their economies and low competitiveness.

Three of the four examined countries received financial resources from the EU countries[3] in the aftermath of the 2008–2009 financial crisis, and the arguments for the disbursements may offer more insights. Greece received financial help between 2010 and 2018 to eliminate structural disparities, mainly in the general government sector (the size of social expenditure), and to be able to finance its growing debt service at that time (European Commission, 2022). Portugal received financial help between 2011 and 2014 to restructure its banking sector, undergo structural reforms, and restore its competitiveness (ibid.). Spain received financial help between 2012 and 2013 to restructure its banking sector (ibid.). Italy did not need financial help. Moreover, as of 2022, the European Central Bank is in schizophrenic position due to the attempts to exit its quantitative easing programmes and help the Southern economies to maintain low interest payments from the government debts. Finally, the countries should also get a higher portion of financial revenues from the common EU budget from 2021 to 2027.

The positions of the countries should also be analysed using composite indicators incorporating various measures. Some of the indicators also utilise qualitative data.[4] Table 6.2 shows 10 selected composite indices[5] of the EU4 countries.

According to the data, Spain likely has the most efficient economy. The next place is split between Italy and Portugal, depending on the used index. Greece is placed last in all the indicators except the first one. Another interesting measure is the estimate of economic freedom. According to these measures, Spain and Portugal are the freest economies out of the EU4 countries.

Furthermore, according to the Economic Complexity Index, Italy has the greatest productive capabilities. Finally, the development of the indices can also provide some information. For instance, the sovereign bond ratings for Greece improved in 2022 despite the COVID-19 and Ukraine war crises as well as the sharp debt accumulation in the EU. Arguably, it was due to complex subsidy programmes

[2]The economic policy measures and '*rescue*' packages were primarily focused on mitigating the worst consequences in the short and medium term. The countries did not solve their structural issues. For instance, Ševčíková (2015) provides an analysis of the problematics.

[3]The EU can be mentioned as a single supranational institution. However, the resources came (mainly) from other countries through payments to the institution. In addition, a part of the financing was also provided by the IMF.

[4]Most prominently the Corruption Perceptions Index and sovereign bond ratings.

[5]There are numerous problems with the intercomparison of these indices. First, the names of their versions usually do not correspond to the year when the data were obtained. Second, their sample sizes differ, making the assessments of relative position in the world more difficult. Third, the used methodologies vary over time in some cases, making the values of the indices not fully comparable in time.

Table 6.2 Selected composite indices related to macroeconomic development—EU4, 2019–2022

Country	Human Development Index 2021	Index of Economic Freedom 2022	Economic Freedom of the World 2020	Ease of Doing Business 2020[a]	Sovereign Bond Ratings 2022
Italy	30/191	57/177	44/165	58/190	Adequate
Spain	27/191	41/177	28/165	31/190	Strong or adequate
Portugal	38/191	31/177	42/165	39/190	Adequate
Greece	33/191	77/177	85/165	79/190	Adequate
Country	World Competitiveness Index 2022	Global Competitiveness Index 2019[b]	Corruption Perceptions Index 2021	Global Innovation Index 2021	Economic Complexity Index 2020
Italy	41/63	30/141	56/180	29/132	16/133
Spain	36/63	23/141	61/180	30/132	33/133
Portugal	42/63	34/141	62/180	31/132	34/133
Greece	47/63	59/141	49/180	47/132	50/133

Note: Bond ratings are taken from Moody's, Standard & Poor's, and Fitch agencies
Source: CID (2022), CU (2022), FI (2022), HF (2022), IMD (2022), TI (2022), TE (2022), UN (2022), WB (2022), WEF (2022), and own processing
[a]In September 2021, World Bank Group management decided to discontinue the report
[b]The Global Competitiveness Report was not published since 2020

(both on the national and supranational levels) and the greater socialisation of risks in the EU.[6]

Figure 6.1 shows the real GDP growth rates of the EU4 countries compared to the average values of the European Union and the Euro Area. The countries' developments significantly diverged between 2008 and 2014, during and in the aftermath of the financial crisis—most notably Greece. Italy and Portugal recorded systematically lower growth values even before 2008. Unfortunately, the overall economic performance of Italy did not significantly change in the examined period. Italy has shown economic stagnation, with economic growth near zero in the last two decades. Moreover, the coronavirus crisis introduced another divergence in 2020 as a reaction to a macroeconomic shock. The EU4 countries showed a more substantial economic decline than the EU and the Euro Area average, which could be the result of the structural flaws in these countries—similar to the previous financial crisis.[7] Nevertheless, the issue is complicated because the lockdowns associated with the coronavirus crisis were country-specific, and the Southern economies suffered more due to their developed tourism sectors.

Furthermore, comparing real GDP growth with estimated output gaps is useful. It is depicted in Fig. 6.2. The EU4 countries were significantly overheated prior to the financial crisis of 2008–2009. The crisis hit was a significant macroeconomic shock

[6]Refer to the discussion about the European debt crisis in the previous chapter.
[7]Refer to the previous chapters.

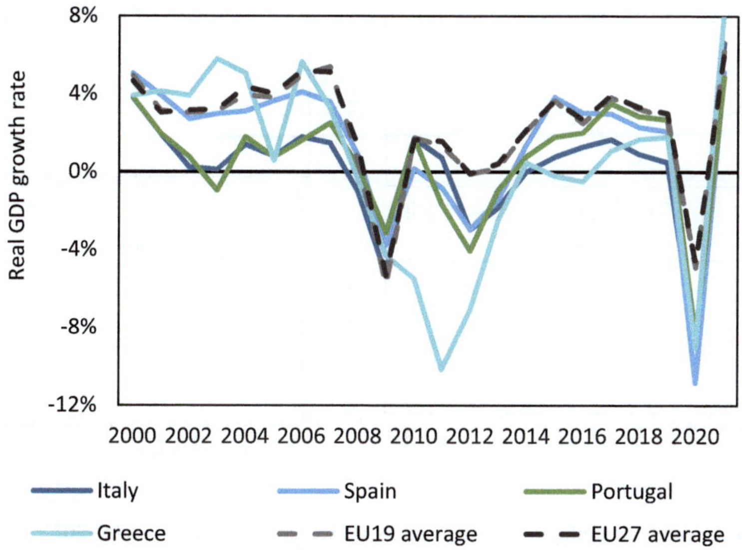

Fig. 6.1 Real GDP developments—Selected EU Countries—2000–2021. Note: Simple arithmetic averages are used. These values are higher than the weighted average values reported by Eurostat. Source: IMF (2022), own calculations and processing

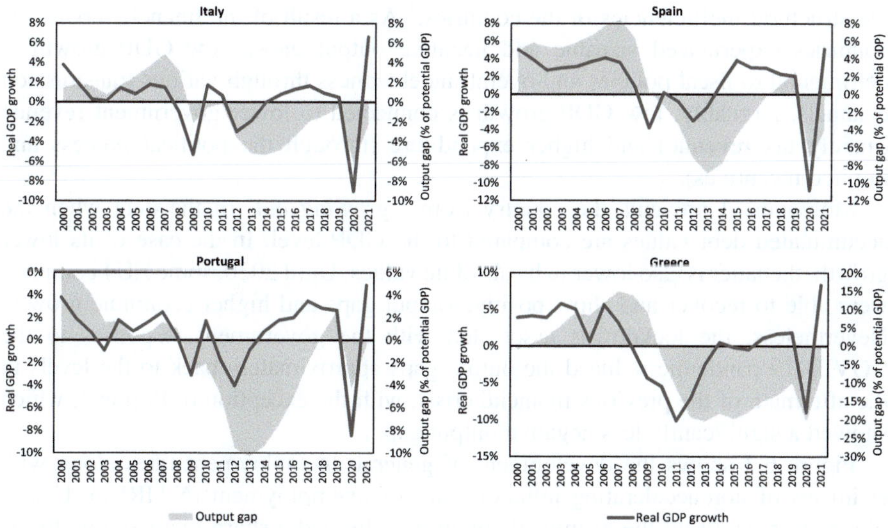

Fig. 6.2 Real GDP growth rates and estimated output gaps—EU4, 2000–2021. Note: The output gaps are estimated by a trivariate unobserved components model presented in the seventh chapter. Source: Eurostat (2022), own calculations and processing

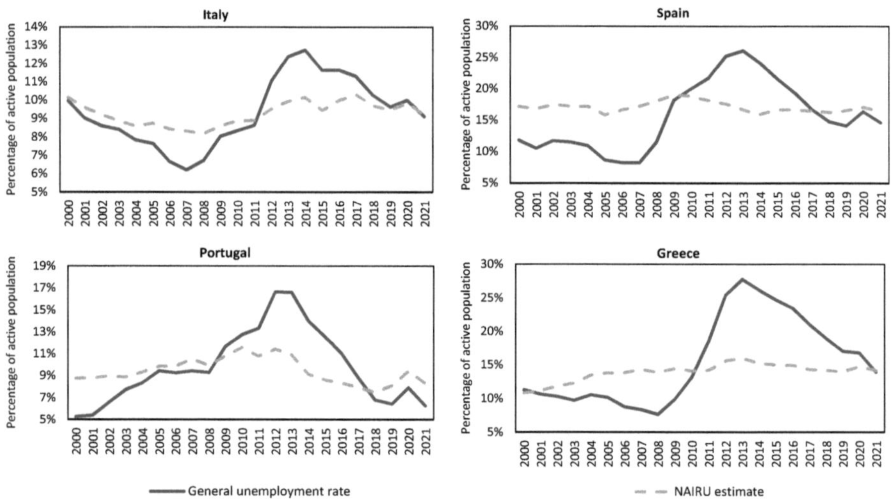

Fig. 6.3 General unemployment rates and NAIRU estimates—EU4, 2000–2021. Note: The Non-Accelerating Inflation Rates of Unemployment (NAIRUs) are estimated by a trivariate unobserved components model presented in the seventh chapter. Source: Eurostat (2022), own calculations and processing

for the countries. Moreover, economic recovery mechanisms were weakened due to the structural inefficiencies of the countries.[8] As a result of the financial crisis, the countries experienced sizeable and negative output gaps. Low GDP growth is detrimental to fiscal policies and overall indebtedness through various transmission channels. Arguably, low GDP growth is connected to lower government revenue (mainly tax revenue) and higher expenditure (through the political process and implied incentives).

Moreover, it prevents the country from ‘ growing *out*’ of the debt when the accumulated debt values are compared to the GDP level. In the case of its lower growth, the latter is also lower in its absolute values. Until 2020, some EU4 countries were able to recover and show positive output gaps and higher economic growth. Nevertheless, the lockdowns associated with the government responses to the COVID-19 pandemic reduced the output gaps approximately back to the levels in the aftermath of the previous financial crisis, with the exception of Portugal, which showed a significantly less negative output gap.

Figure 6.3 shows the development of general unemployment rates along with estimates of non-accelerating inflation rates of unemployment (NAIRUs). Unemployment rates of all the examined countries exhibited a sharp increase due to the financial crisis of 2008–2009. The fact puts pressure on government expenditure through the payments of social benefits and restricts government revenue both

[8]I refer to the sub-optimality of the uniform euro exchange rate.

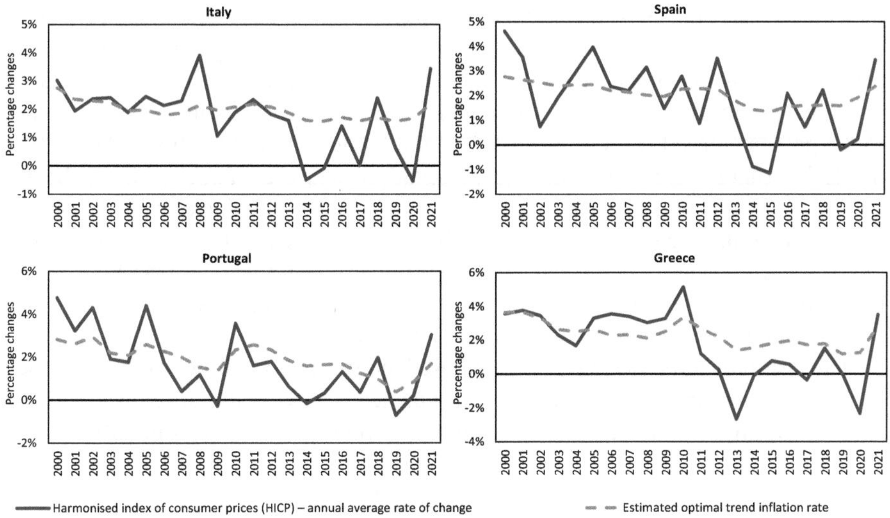

Fig. 6.4 Consumer price level developments and optimal trend inflation rates—EU4, 2000–2021. Note: The optimal trend inflation rates are estimated by a trivariate unobserved components model presented in the seventh chapter. Source: Eurostat (2022), own calculations and processing

directly and indirectly.[9] In addition, the results show stagnation or an increase in the NAIRU estimates depending on the country, which indicated strong labour market rigidities in these economies. The observation is at odds with the global trend of decreases in the NAIRUs in advanced economies. The fact can be interpreted as both cause and consequence of the significant decrease in economic efficiency and competitiveness of the countries.

Nevertheless, the NAIRU estimates are subject to the changing economic environment and are directly influenced by prolonged periods of expansionary economic policies, which many economists often overlook. Since 2013–2014, the unemployment rates gradually declined, making the unemployment gaps lower, possibly resulting from higher economic growth. Arguably, the rigidities were not eliminated. Hence, we might expect another dynamic development in the future due to the COVID-19 crisis. Unemployment rates are indicators with relatively high inertia, and, in some cases, they might significantly lag behind economic growth and structural changes.

Figure 6.4 depicts the average annual changes of the harmonised index of consumer prices (HICP) along with estimated optimal trend inflation rates[10] of the EU4 countries. It should be noted that the environment has been disinflationary until

[9]The direct effect means lower income tax revenues, while the indirect effects are connected to lower economic efficiency due to the sub-optimal use of resources in the economy.

[10]This type of inflation rate is defined as the measure, which is maximising steady-state economic welfare. Nevertheless, the notion of '*optimal*' inflation rate is inherently problematic due to the

the coronavirus crisis. Arguably, this fact has been caused by various factors. These include the current economic situation of the countries,[11] tightening of financial regulation, loss of competitiveness, market competition in the EU27, overall technological progress, low oil prices, relatively high demand saturation when compared to the past, increased risks or uncertainty, and liquidity trap conditions. After 2019, the EU4 countries recorded significant inflation pressures along with all the EU countries. These pressures appeared because of economic lockdowns associated with lowered aggregate supply (the number of businesses and the portfolio of their goods and services declined) and postponed aggregate demand pressures (unavailability of goods created surplus savings which were later spent) in combination with expansionary fiscal[12] and monetary policies.[13]

The last indicators that should be analysed are the external flows of the countries. It can be shown that the current account balance (CAB) is the difference between savings (S) and investments (I) in an open economy (refer to Eurostat, 2013):

$$\mathrm{CAB} = S - I$$

Current account balances are shown in Fig. 6.5 and represent one of the stylised facts of the past. The values confirm the twin deficit hypothesis in the EU4 countries. The hypothesis claims a strong causal link between a nation's government budget balance and its current account balance. The EU4 countries exhibited acute deficits in their current accounts in the past, which arguably destabilised their economies.[14] The imbalances were mainly caused by the euro-debt mechanism, moral hazard, and expansionary macroeconomic policies. The structural difference in the EU is directly observable when the EU4 countries are compared to the average values of the EU core countries, Euro Area, and European Union. In line with the previous insights,[15] the deficits disappeared after 2013 in all the EU4 countries except Greece. Note that this country recorded prolonged deficits after 2020 again.

Furthermore, it is crucial to identify the institutional sector developments in the case of external balances. A viable measure of the situation is net lending/net borrowing, which is used as the overall budget balance measure in the case of the general government sector. The net lending/net borrowing (NL/NB) is defined as the

complex relationships of the inflation rate with other main macroeconomic variables. It is presented for illustrative purposes only.

[11] High indebtedness with less space for aggregate demand to further stimulate inflation.

[12] Both on the national and supranational levels. The EU increased its common budget resources for the period of 2021–2027 by approximately 80%, which represented the Next Generation EU package.

[13] For a detailed discussion, refer to Zubíková and Smolák (2022).

[14] A more detailed analysis should be focused on the structural development of the current accounts. However, the aim is to present the essential facts in a concise manner.

[15] It was also due to '*recovery programmes*' and related regulations, which were associated with financial assistance from the EU.

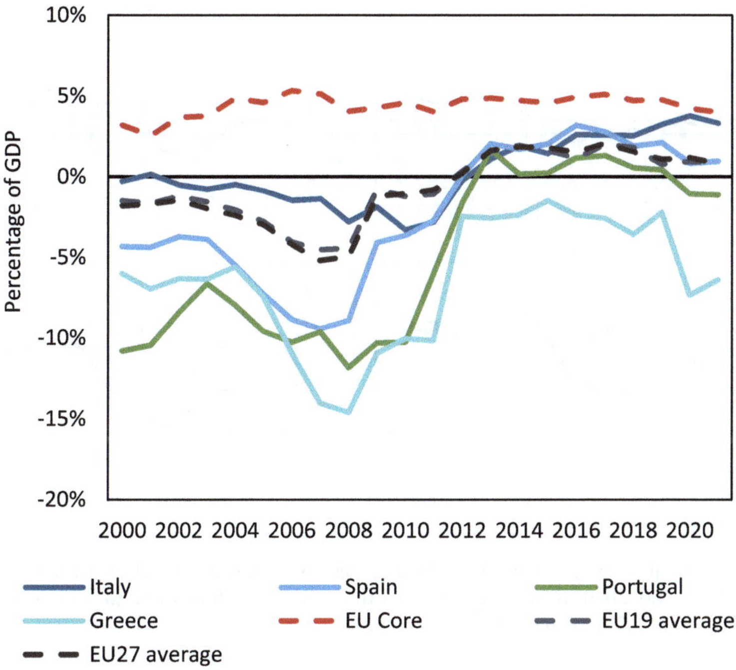

Fig. 6.5 Current account balances—selected EU countries, GDP ratios—2000–2021. Notes: Simple arithmetic averages are used. The EU Core countries group consists of Germany, Austria, the Netherlands, and Luxembourg. Source: IMF (2022), own calculations and processing

current account balance (CAB) adjusted for net capital transfers (NCT)[16] realised in the economy (refer to Eurostat, 2013):

$$NL/NB = CAB + NCT$$

A sectoral decomposition of the total economy's net lending/net borrowing can be made using the data from the national accounts.[17] It is shown in Fig. 6.6. I separate general government sectors and compare them with the aggregates of all the other sectors (households and companies). The results show that the general government sector was a source of severe economic instabilities after 2009 in all the examined countries. It puts pressure on the current level of government debt and restricts[18] economic growth—magnifying its effects over time. The highest negative values (lending) of the general government sectors were recorded in Greece, Spain,

[16]To be precise, the acquisitions and less disposals of non-financial non-produced assets should also be added. However, the size of this item is negligible.

[17]The EU countries use the European System of National and Regional Accounts (ESA 2010) framework, which is a derivative of the System of National Accounts (SNA 2008).

[18]Under the assumption of a considerably high debt level.

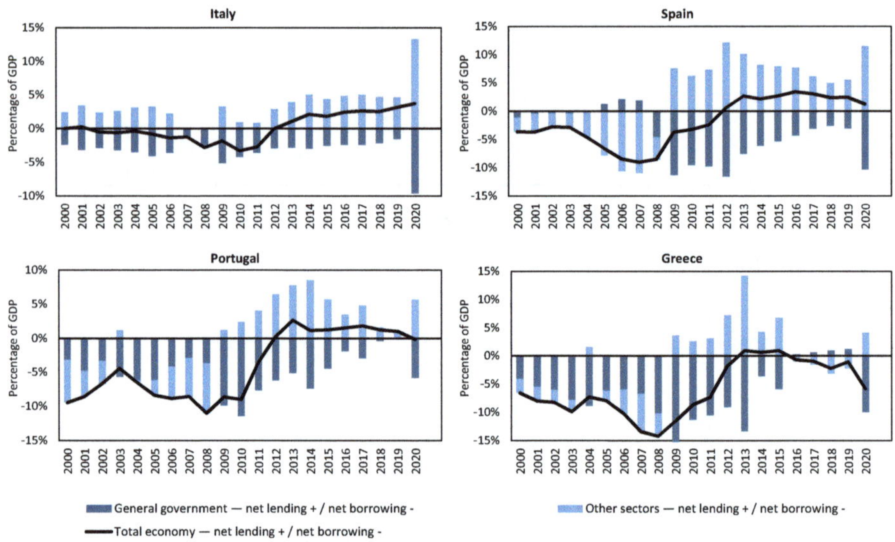

Fig. 6.6 Sectoral decomposition of net lending/net borrowing in the selected economies, GDP ratios—EU4, 2000–2020. Note: The presented time series are shorter due to data unavailability. Source: Eurostat (2022), own calculations and processing

and Portugal. Even though Italy is showing chronic government deficits, its sizes were relatively small until the COVID-19 crisis.

To conclude, the EU4 countries experienced significant economic turbulences after the recession, partly caused by inappropriate macroeconomic policies—both on the national and supranational levels. It was reflected in sizeably negative output gaps, high unemployment rates, external disbalances, and accumulated debt levels.

6.2 Positions of the Countries in the EU

I employ cluster analysis in the following text to obtain a broader view of the EU countries' positions. Cluster analysis (or clustering) is a useful tool to examine complex relations among countries without imposing any a priori restrictions on the interrelationships.[19] As a result, the method may serve as a complementary analysis to various regression models (functions) that need to be specified (Kok & Puigvert Gutiérrez, 2006).

The literature dealing with cluster analysis of the EU countries is extensive. The analyses are determined by the methodology used, types of variables, sample size, and time frame. For example, Belke et al. (2016) and Ahlborn and Wortmann (2018)

[19]The results are driven by the data in the context of the methodology used. Nevertheless, the clustering exercise may be done using various methods.

focused on European business cycles, Burian and Frydrych (2017) examined economic convergence, Zwick and Syed (2017) dealt with labour markets, Cesaroni et al. (2019) examined income inequality, and Kok and Puigvert Gutiérrez (2006) focused on the banking sector. The research of Artis and Zhang (2002) or Wortmann and Stahl (2016) can be mentioned as it deals with general characteristics among the Euro Area countries. The results of the analyses mostly confirmed the hypothesis that EU4 countries form a separate cluster.

Box 6.1 Cluster Analysis of the EU4 Countries Positions: Used Methodology

I use the most applied clustering method in economics: an agglomerative hierarchical cluster analysis.[20] The approach is based on a distance matrix used for (dis)similarity evaluation of all pairs of objects. The process gradually builds up from the bottom, merging countries into separate clusters until all the countries are agglomerated into a single cluster.

First, the data must be transformed before the clustering algorithm processes them. Variables with a larger scale would have a more significant impact in each cluster without data standardisation. Instead of a z-score, however, I use an alternative standardisation. The applied standardisation is a more robust measure because its denominator is more sensible to observations far away from the centre (Kok & Puigvert Gutiérrez, 2006, p. 10):

$$X_s = \frac{X - X_{\min}}{X_{\max} - X_{\min}}.$$

Then, I calculate the medians for all the indicators in a particular time frame for each country. I have decided not to use average values because of erratic fluctuations in the data. Furthermore, I use Euclidean distance regarding the cluster (dis)similarity evaluation because it places greater emphasis on outliers to generate distance patterns. I presume that distinctions in the data should be formed on the basis of outliers.

Finally, a linkage method regarding the clustering algorithm needs to be chosen. No single approach can be considered the '*most appropriate*'. Therefore, I have chosen Ward's clustering procedure because it produces empirically plausible results. The procedure seeks to form partitions in a manner that minimises the loss of information associated with each merging; hence Ward's method is often referred to as the '*minimum-variance method*'. An intragroup sum of squares of differences in values from the cluster average is used as the

(continued)

[20] There are two main reasons for the claim. First, the number of final clusters is often unknown. Second, agglomerative methods are widely implemented in statistical software.

Box 6.1 (continued)
homogeneity measure, called Ward's criterion. It is denoted G_1 and calculated as follows (Ward, 1963, p. 237):

$$G_1 = \sum_{h=1}^{k} \sum_{i=1}^{n_h} \sum_{j=1}^{t} \left(X_{hij} - \overline{X}_{hj}\right)^2,$$

where k is the number of clusters, n_h is the number of objects in the hth cluster, and t is the number of variables describing objects. Ward's criterion then minimises the subsequent expression to facilitate that there is a minimal increase in G_1 in each clustering step (Ward, 1963, p. 237):

$$\Delta G_1 = \sum_{i=1}^{g} \sum_{j=1}^{t} \left(X_{gij} - \overline{X}_{gj}\right)^2 - \sum_{i=1}^{h} \sum_{j=1}^{t} \left(X_{hij} - \overline{X}_{hj}\right)^2 - \sum_{i=1}^{h'} \sum_{j=1}^{t} \left(X_{h'ij} - \overline{X}_{h'j}\right)^2.$$

The outputs of the analysis are presented in the form of dendrograms, illustrating the arrangement of produced clusters.

The main goal is to identify outliers (country groups) in the EU27, EU19, and EU4, emphasising the EU4 countries and their structural development between 2000 and 2019. The period after 2020 is purposely not used because of the lockdowns, which were not a result of market processes but rather a result of country-specific political decisions. These regulations significantly affect the data. I examined different combinations of 40 variables that should representatively describe the economies. These include GDP and GDP per capita characteristics, sectoral development, international trade, labour market and demographic development, price development, research and development, indicators of general government sector indebtedness, real exchange rate, and labour cost developments. In the end, I selected 29 variables that provide plausible results regarding the chosen methodology. I presume that the clustering algorithm must be able to separate less and more developed countries and possibly identify the Southern wing of the EU as one of the outliers.

I have purposely selected indices that are not strictly determined by the size of the economies.[21] The analysis focuses on the countries' structural characteristics, which are mainly represented by relative values. The need for including these structural characteristics is evident when evaluating the EU4 countries, which significantly

[21] It does not mean that the economic size has no effect. However, it is arguably not the primary factor in the case of most of the selected variables.

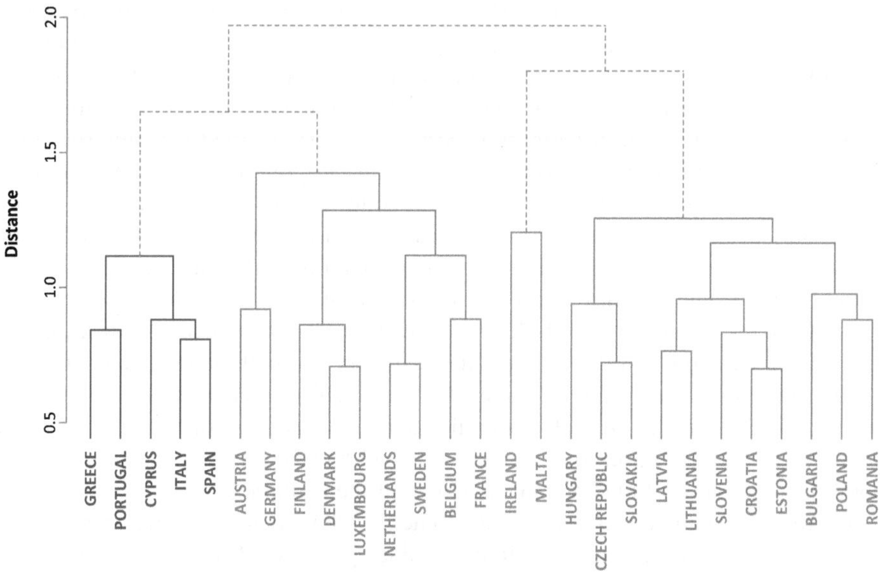

Fig. 6.7 Cluster analysis (Ward's method)—EU27, 2000–2019. Source: Own calculations and processing

differ in economic size, but share common characteristics. Moreover, the analysis puts relatively more emphasis on GDP structures and their development. Note that the analysis may also indicate the fulfilment of the OCA criteria when comparing the individual countries to the core countries—for example, the German cluster. Finally, I have used an identical methodology for each sample size and period combination to keep the research outcome as robust as possible.[22]

6.3 Country Positions in the European Union

According to the presented results, the EU4 countries can be considered a specific and separate group of countries in the EU and the Euro Area. Therefore, the countries should be concurrently analysed because of their structural similarities. Historically, the countries belonging to the group are more developed countries that did not experience the period of communism (socialism in practice). The relevant dendrogram is presented in Fig. 6.7, which shows a cluster analysis of all the EU countries between 2000 and 2019. The algorithm distinguishes highly developed economies, less developed economies, and selected Southern countries (wing) of the EU. Moreover, it puts together countries that are geographically and culturally

[22]It should also be mentioned that, by definition, the cluster organisation is unstable in the cases of highly volatile changes. I needed to make some expert adjustments.

similar. The '*German*' and the '*French*' wing within the more advanced EU countries is apparent in many cases. Italy, Spain, Portugal, Greece, and Cyprus[23] were identified as a separate cluster within the more advanced EU countries between 2000 and 2019. It indicates that the countries form relatively distinct regions.

Moreover, analyses of different time periods suggest that the EU4 countries form a relatively stable cluster because it held even in the pre-crisis and financial crisis periods. A sizeable economic shock offers robust evidence as it usually forces economic specifics to show up[24]—this was the case with the financial crisis of 2008–2009.[25] In other cases, however, considerably different countries (under normal circumstances) may show higher similarity due to a common negative external shock. The period of 2017–2019 showed some changes, making the distinctions less apparent due to economic recovery and both national and supranational economic policy stimulus in the EU. The situation after made the distinctions even more difficult. It promoted significant macroeconomic differences in some areas (variables). However, the country-wide lockdowns were very specific and did not reflect the inherent market characteristics of the countries.

Finally, it should be mentioned that another Southern country—France, probably does not belong to the group of the four examined countries. The are several possible implications connected to the structural difference of France: disparate linkages to other countries, different historical development, cultural specifics, and other factors.

6.4 Country Positions in the Euro Area

A narrower analysis of the Euro Area (EU19 or EMU) between 2000 and 2019 leads to similar conclusions as in the previous case. The algorithm distinguishes between advanced and less advanced economies. Nevertheless, the EU4 countries are possibly closer to the less advanced economies within the Euro Area. The results are shown in Fig. 6.8.

Furthermore, formal tests of the optimal number of clusters indicate similar or slightly lower fragmentation of the EU19 countries compared to the EU27. According to the tests, the Euro Area was more fragmented before the financial crisis. The EU4 countries formed a distinct cluster during all of the sub-periods of 2000–2019, except for Spain in 2017–2019. The fact is difficult to interpret because it can result from the common monetary policy and the socialisation of risks in the Euro Area.

---

[23] The relative economic size of Cyprus is negligible, and it experiences political clashes on the island. For this reason, the country was not included in the analysis.

[24] With the exception of very specific shocks when the origin of the shock is significantly administratively influenced. The countries experienced such a shock after 2019 as a result of the coronavirus pandemic.

[25] I identified 2010 as the '*cut-off*' year.

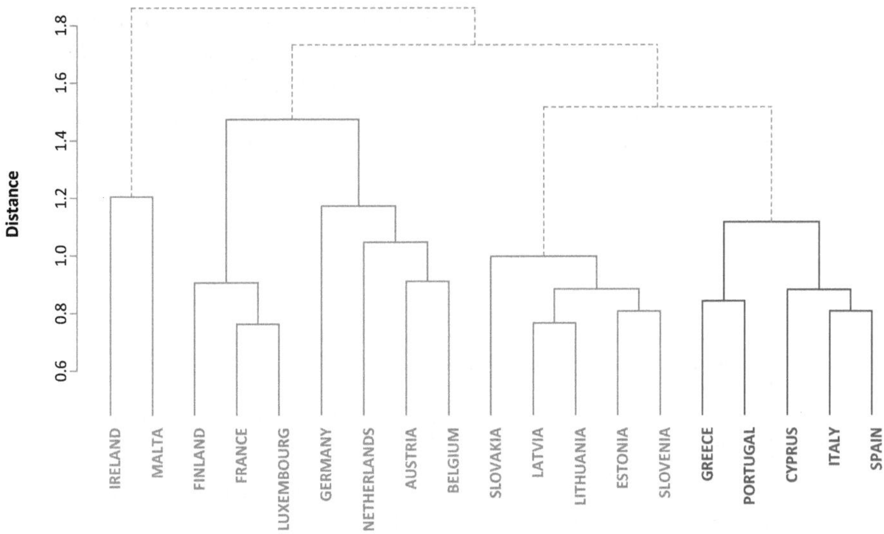

Fig. 6.8 Cluster analysis (Ward's method)—EU19, 2000–2019. Source: Own calculations and processing

Fig. 6.9 Cluster analysis (Ward's method)—EU4, 2000–2019. Source: Own calculations and processing

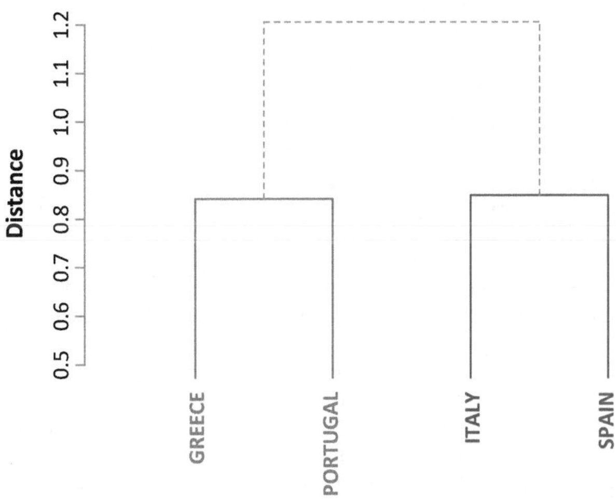

6.5 EU4 Positions in Relation to Each Other

The cluster analysis of EU4 between 2000 and 2019 produced two separate clusters. The results are presented in Fig. 6.9. Therefore, the EU4 countries can be further distinguished into two groups. The fact reflects one of the most important characteristics of the economies: the size of the examined economies. Greece is connected with Portugal, while Italy and Spain are more distinct as a larger group of economies.

An additional analysis of different time periods suggests that the situation was not always stable. Greece, Portugal, and Italy were initially in the same cluster between 2000 and 2009. However, Italy was put into a separate cluster during 2010–2016 due to the financial crisis. Paradoxically, the EU4 country group became more fragmented after the financial crisis.

References

Ahlborn, M., & Wortmann, M. (2018). The core–periphery pattern of European business cycles: A fuzzy clustering approach. *Journal of Macroeconomics, 55*, 12–27. https://doi.org/10.1016/j.jmacro.2017.08.002

Artis, M., & Zhang, W. (2002). Membership of EMU: A fuzzy clustering analysis of alternative criteria. *Journal of Economic Integration, 17*(1), 54–79. Retrieved April 15, 2022, from http://www.jstor.org/stable/23000793

Belke, A. H., Domnick, C., & Gros, D. (2016). *Business cycle synchronization in the EMU: Core vs. periphery* (Ruhr Economic Paper No. 427). CEPS Working Paper. Retrieved March 20, 2022, from https://www.ceps.eu/wp-content/uploads/2016/11/WD427.pdf

Burian, S., & Frydrych, J. (2017). Is there convergence across European countries? Simple cluster analysis approach. *Ekonomický časopis, 65*(5), 393–407.

Center for International Development (CID) — Harvard Kennedy School. (2022). *Economic Complexity Index*. Retrieved August 21, 2022, from https://atlas.cid.harvard.edu/rankings

Cesaroni, T., D'Elia, E., & Santis, R. D. (2019). Inequality in EMU: Is there a core periphery dualism? *The Journal of Economic Asymmetries, 20*(e00121). https://doi.org/10.1016/j.jeca.2019.e00121

Cornell University (CU). (2022). *Global Innovation Index*. Retrieved August 21, 2022, from https://www.globalinnovationindex.org/analysis-indicator

European Commission. (2022). *EU financial assistance*. Retrieved August 05, 2022, from https://ec.europa.eu/info/business-economy-euro/economic-and-fiscal-policy-coordination/eu-financial-assistance/

Eurostat. (2013). *European System of Accounts: ESA 2010* (Manual and Guideline KS-02-13-269-EN-C). European Union. https://doi.org/10.2785/16644

Eurostat. (2022). *Eurostat database*. Retrieved September 21, 2022, from https://ec.europa.eu/eurostat

Fraser Institute (FI). (2022). *Economic Freedom of the World Index*. Retrieved August 21, 2022, from https://www.fraserinstitute.org/economic-freedom

Heritage Foundation (HF). (2022). *Index of Economic Freedom*. Retrieved August 21, 2022, from https://www.heritage.org/index/ranking

International Institute for Management Development (IMD). (2022). *World Competitiveness Index*. Retrieved August 21, 2022, from https://www.imd.org/wcc/world-competitiveness-center-rankings/countries-profiles/

International Monetary Fund (IMF). (2022). *World Economic Outlook Database*. Retrieved August 15, 2022, from https://www.imf.org/en/Publications/WEO

Kok, C., & Puigvert Gutiérrez, J. M. (2006). *Euro Area banking sector integration: Using hierarchical cluster analysis techniques* (ECB Working Paper No. 627). European Central Bank. Retrieved March 2, 2022, from https://www.ecb.europa.eu/pub/pdf/scpwps/ecbwp627.pdf

Organisation for Economic Co-operation and Development (OECD). (2005). *OECD Economic Surveys: Greece 2005* (Tech. Rep.). Retrieved April 20, 2022, from https://www.oecd-ilibrary.org/economics/oecd-economic-surveys-greece-2005_eco_surveys-grc-2005-en

Ševčíková, M. (2015). *Five crises of the European integration process*. Oeconomica, University of Economics, Prague. ISBN: 978-80-245-2098-8.

Trading Economics (TE). (2022). *Country credit ratings*. Retrieved August 21, 2022, from https://tradingeconomics.com/country-list/rating

Transparency International (TI). (2022). *Corruption Perceptions Index*. Retrieved August 21, 2022, from http://cpi.transparency.org/

United Nations (UN). (2022). *Human Development Index (HDI)*. Retrieved August 21, 2022, from http://hdr.undp.org/en/content/human-development-index-hdi

Ward, J. H., Jr. (1963). Hierarchical grouping to optimize an objective function. *Journal of the American Statistical Association, 58*(301), 236–244. https://doi.org/10.1080/01621459.1963.10500845

World Bank (WB). (2022). *Ease of Doing Business Index*. Retrieved August 21, 2022, from https://www.doingbusiness.org/

World Economic Forum (WEF). (2022). *Global Competitiveness Index*. Retrieved August 21, 2022, from https://www.weforum.org/reports/global-competitiveness-report-2019

Wortmann, M., & Stahl, M. (2016). One size fits some: A reassessment of EMU's core-periphery framework. *Journal of Economic Integration, 31*(2), 377–413. http://www.jstor.org/stable/43783271

Zubíková, A., & Smolák, P. (2022). Macroeconomic impacts of the COVID-19 pandemic in the Czech Republic in the period of 2020-2021. *International Journal of Economic Sciences, 11*(1), 117–145. https://doi.org/10.52950/es.2022.11.1.008

Zwick, H. S., & Syed, S. A. S. (2017). The polarization impact of the crisis on the Eurozone labour markets: A hierarchical cluster analysis. *Applied Economics Letters, 24*(7), 472–476. https://doi.org/10.1080/13504851.2016.1203055

Chapter 7
Fiscal Situation in the COVID-19 Aftermath

The starting point for any fiscal analysis is the historical development of fiscal policies and their implications. The examination has several dimensions. First, both flow and stock indicators need to be examined. Second, the analyses utilise estimated and actual data. Some of the analysed factors can sometimes be considerably volatile. However, this chapter focuses on identifying relatively stable patterns. The findings will provide general information about the fiscal conditions of the selected countries.

The chapter has three main parts. First, it shows the main fiscal indicators of the EU4 countries. The measures have limited explanatory power but are based on directly observed data. Second, it presents estimates of structural budget balances, examines their development, and derives characteristics of the EU4 fiscal policies. The results are compared to the estimates of major international institutions—the IMF, OECD, and European Commission. Several estimates need to be performed to be able to extract relevant information. The text describes the procedures used. Third, it evaluates the countries' positions from a long-term view using a fiscal sustainability analysis.

7.1 Main Fiscal Indicators

The analysis begins with an examination of various descriptive measures capturing the fiscal situation of the countries. I start with the broadest measures and proceed to more detailed indicators. It should be noted that some data, especially for Greece, are not publicly available. Therefore, I approximated the values or used alternative sources when it was possible. Moreover, the following text presents three groups of the examined measures: headline indicators, variables capturing debt structure, and selected benchmark indicators. Finally, it focuses on both the frequency (flow vs stock indicators) and time dimension (short- vs long-term indicators).

M. Bednář, *Fiscal Policy in the Southern European Union Countries*, Contributions to Finance and Accounting, https://doi.org/10.1007/978-3-031-29761-8_7

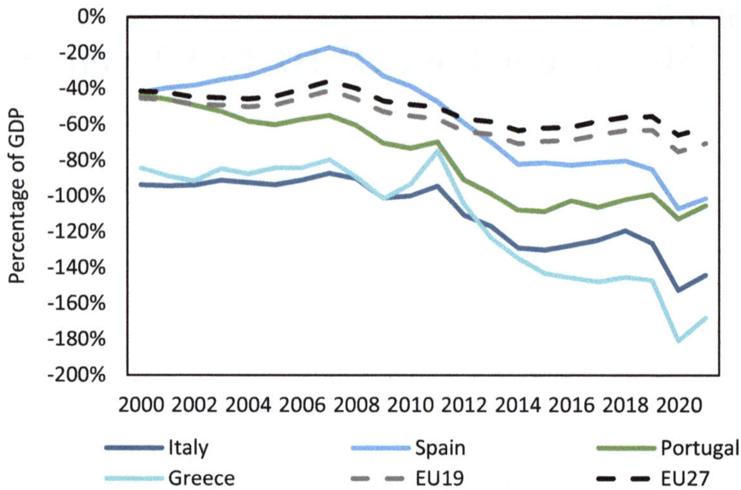

Fig. 7.1 General government net financial wealth, GDP ratios—EU4, 2000–2021. Source: Eurostat (2022a), own processing

7.1.1 Headline Indicators

Possibly one of the broadest measures is the general government net wealth (or net worth) indicator which shows the differences between financial assets and outstanding liabilities held by the government. It summarises the government's ability to fully honour its obligations and can also be viewed as a broad measure of net government debt (OECD, 2017). The worsening of this indicator is directly connected to the deterioration of the government's fiscal position in terms of sustainability. Nevertheless, the vast majority of countries show negative values because they are significantly indebted, meaning their liabilities are higher than their assets.[1] For instance, the average value for the Organisation for Economic Co-operation and Development (OECD) countries was −29.6% in 2021 (OECD, 2022).

Figure 7.1 shows the situation of the EU4 countries, along with the European Union (EU27) and the Euro Area (EU19). First, the initial positions of Spain and Portugal were relatively favourable until 2008, until they started to decline sharply. Most notably, the situation of Spain was even more favourable than the EU aggregates. Second, the positions of Greece and Italy were already unfavourable in 2000. Later, the countries showed a much sharper decline after the recession due to a negative snowball effect. In contrast, the positions of the EU27 and the EU19 were also declining; however, it was relatively stable and developing slowly. Finally, the

[1]There are a few exceptions; for example, Norway showed a positive value of 354% of its GDP in 2021 because of its relatively low indebtedness and significant financial assets stemming from the possession of natural resources.

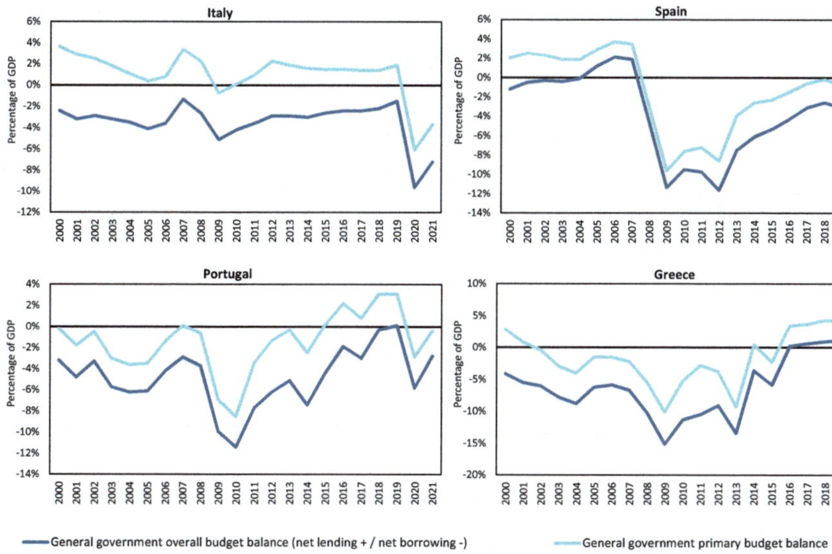

Fig. 7.2 Overall and primary balance of general government sector, GDP ratios—EU4, 2000–2021. Source: Eurostat (2022a), own calculations and processing

EU4 countries are showing one of the worst values even in the world context. For example, Greece, with −167.4%, placed last among all the OECD countries (OECD, 2022).

It was already shown in the previous chapter that the EU4 countries' government balances were sources of significant economies instabilities. The overall budget balances, along with primary balance indicators, are presented in Fig. 7.2. The two measures are crucial for a proper interpretation of the occurring. The data show that, on average, all the EU4 countries ran non-negligible budget deficits. It should be mentioned that Spain reached a roughly balanced overall budget measure until the financial crisis. In addition, Italy was characterised by chronic budget deficits for all the examined periods. However, the deficits were relatively small when compared to the other countries. Note that the position of Italy could have been misinterpreted if it was based only on the interpretation of the overall budget balance indicators. The country suffered from relatively high interest payments on government debt. The country was running budget surpluses after deducting the payments from the overall budget balance measure.[2] The developments in Portugal and Greece were conceptually similar. Nonetheless, the latter country showed higher volatility.

Figure 7.3 depicts the overall general government gross and net debt to GDP ratios. The EU4 countries are currently among the most indebted countries in the world. In 2021, Greece was the third most indebted country in the world, measured

[2]It is represented by the primary budget balance measure. Note that the deduction of payments is a double minus, which translates into arithmetic addition.

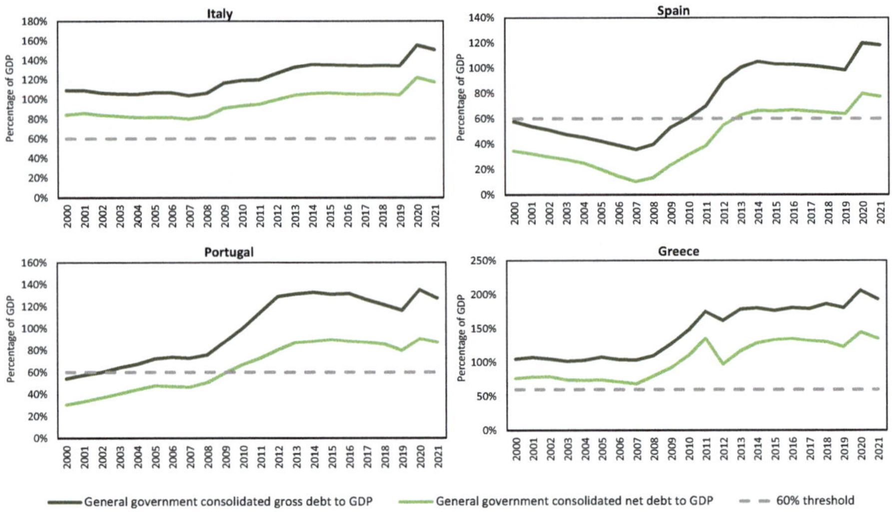

Fig. 7.3 General government gross and net debt, GDP ratios—EU4, 2000–2021. Notes: Net government debt depicted above is calculated by subtracting total general government financial assets from the gross debt indicator. The 2021 net debt value for Italy was calculated based on financial assets from 2020 due to data unavailability. Source: Eurostat (2022a), own calculations and processing

by general government gross debt to GDP ratios, after Venezuela and Japan. Moreover, in terms of being the most indebted countries in the world, Italy ranked 7th, Portugal ranked 13th, and Spain ranked 17th (see IMF, 2022). Furthermore, I included a horizontal line marking the 60% debt-to-GDP ratio in Fig. 7.3 to capture the corresponding Maastricht criterion limit. The data show that the debt ratios sharply increased after 2008, stabilised between 2014 and 2019, and sharply increased in 2020. All of the countries significantly exceeded the Maastricht criterion limit. Furthermore, the differences between gross and net debts are relatively small and do not influence the interpretation of the occurrence.

Interest payments on general government debt are shown separately in Fig. 7.4. The measure is more precise than the Maastricht long-term interest rate criterion because it is a broader indicator. The interest payments on debt were historically more significant for Greece and Italy than for the other two examined countries. The contrast was, to some extent, a result of the differences in the risk profiles of the countries.

Nevertheless, the situation after 2010 drastically changed. There is a noticeable divergence in the developments between 2008 and 2013 due to the financial crisis. Later, the quantitative easing programme (among other factors) of the ECB pushed the interest rates together, and the countries showed relatively small differences compared to past development. These levels, undoubtedly, do not reflect the macroeconomic fundamentals of the countries. They rather represent the result of the

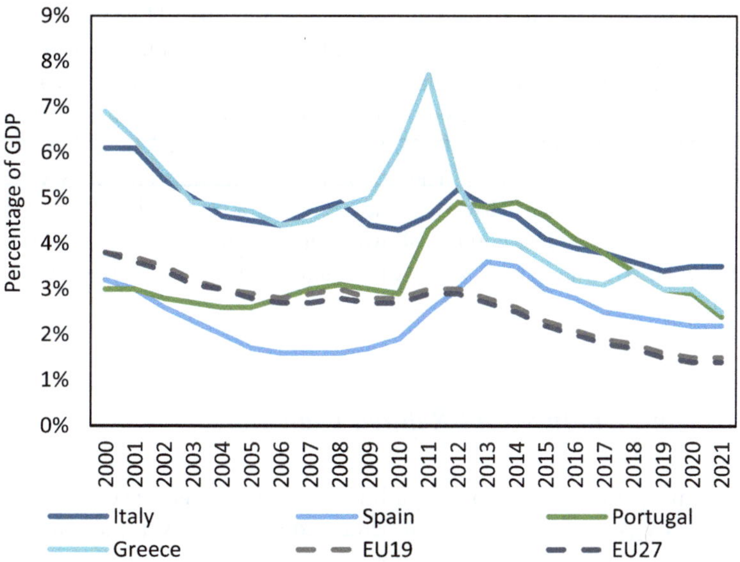

Fig. 7.4 Interest payments on government debt, GDP ratios—EU4, 2000–2021. Source: Eurostat (2022a), own processing

Table 7.1 Total outstanding liabilities of government-controlled entities classified outside general governments (non-consolidated), GDP ratios—EU4, 2013–2020

Year	EU27 average	EU19 average	Italy	Spain	Portugal	Greece
2013	39.0%	45.3%	45.5%	12.5%	51.8%	6.8%
2014	41.1%	47.3%	44.3%	37.8%	79.3%	15.4%
2015	41.1%	47.4%	47.4%	29.6%	72.8%	91.4%
2016	43.4%	53.1%	51.9%	25.7%	66.2%	144.3%
2017	40.4%	48.6%	55.6%	23.0%	38.2%	119.6%
2018	36.6%	43.1%	52.8%	21.0%	34.3%	119.9%
2019	36.4%	42.8%	54.9%	20.0%	33.8%	124.3%
2020	37.7%	38.0%	65.0%	22.6%	38.2%	170.6%

Source: Eurostat (2022a), own processing

socialisation of risks in the Euro Area.[3] As of 2021, all EU4 countries show higher payments than the European Union and the Euro Area averages.

Lastly, the total outstanding liabilities of government-controlled entities are depicted in Table 7.1. These liabilities influence the level of public debt and are not captured within the general government sector. Unfortunately, the presented data are not consolidated, and the respective values covering the whole examined period are unavailable. Hence, it should be interpreted with caution.

[3] Refer to the previous chapters.

As of 2020, only Spain showed a lower value than the EU aggregates. Portugal was able to reduce the level of outstanding liabilities significantly in the past, but the COVID-19 crisis resulted in a slightly higher value than the average. In addition, Italy's liabilities gradually increased over time and were above the EU19 average by approximately 27 percentage points. Greece can be considered an outlier with a very progressive dynamic after 2014. The country's outstanding liabilities were practically non-existent in 2013. However, they reached a prohibitive level of approximately 170% in 2020. The country showed an increment of almost 50 percentage points between 2019 and 2020, which has arguably, further increased the Greek risk premium.

7.1.2 Debt Structure and Related Indicators

One of the most critical indicators regarding debt structure is the composition of debt holders. It provides information about perceived risks or government interventions. The data are more demanding on the input information; therefore, it is often difficult to obtain them. In this case, they were collected from the respective EU4 national sources. Nevertheless, it was not possible to obtain the same division for Greece. The Greek Public Debt Management Agency (PDMA) is the only official source that provides relevant information publicly, but it does not distinguish between residents and non-residents. Hence, the data for Greece reflect the private-public sectoral composition only.

Eurostat (2022a) provides values for most of the EU countries. The EU average may serve as a benchmark. In 2021, the EU26 countries (EU countries without Greece due to data unavailability) showed that non-residents held 46% of their general government gross debts. However, the values were notably diverse among the countries. For instance, Cyprus recorded the highest value—89.4% of its debt was held by non-residents, while Sweden showed the lowest value of only 19.1% (ibid.).

The data for the EU4 countries are depicted in Fig. 7.5. First, Spain and Italy have been historically below average when considering non-residential debt holders. The fact can be considered a positive contribution to their situation. Second, the data show some significant changes after 2008. However, most of them have been pronounced solely in Greece. Since 2012, the Greek general government's gross debt has been held predominantly by the public sector due to government interventions. It can be argued that this indicator already suggests that the country de facto bankrupted because the private sector perceived the risks as prohibitively high and decided not to participate in the new debt emissions (or holdings). The private sector shares are much higher in the other EU4 countries. Moreover, the data for resident/non-resident holdings for Greece are not publicly available, but it is possible to assume that the non-residential holdings are very high and above the EU average.

Another crucial characteristic is the share of foreign currency-denominated debts. High foreign currency-denominated debt shares are problematic when a serious

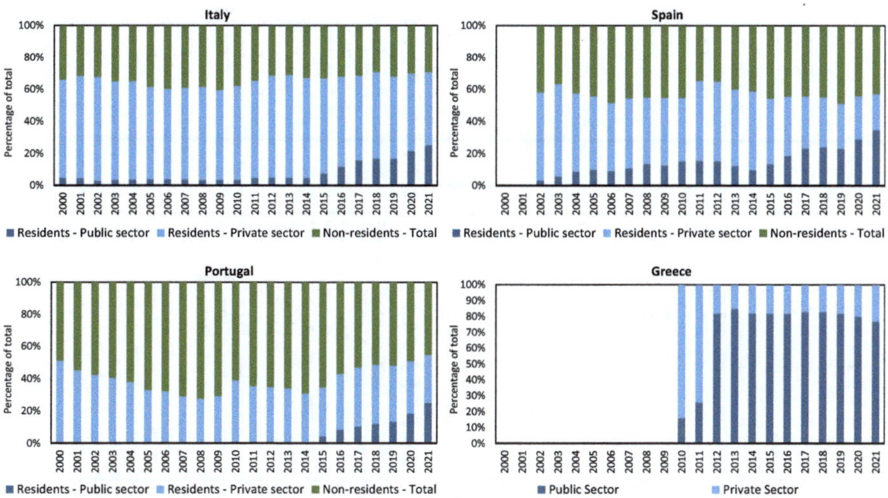

Fig. 7.5 General government gross debt decomposition—debt holders by residency, shares of total—EU4, 2000–2021. Note: The data for Greece reflect the private-public sectoral composition only due to data unavailability. Source: Bank of Italy (2022), Bank of Portugal (2022), PDMA Greece (2022), and Spanish Ministry of Finance (2022), own calculations and processing

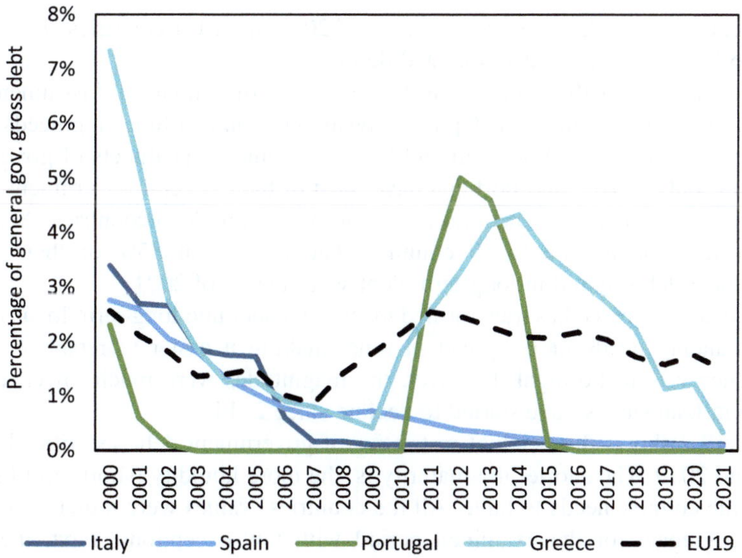

Fig. 7.6 General government gross debt denominated in foreign currencies—shares of total—EU4, 2000–2021. Source: ECB (2022), own calculations and processing

domestic currency depreciation occurs. Figure 7.6 shows that the respective shares of the EU4 countries are negligible. Arguably, the main reason is the adoption of the common euro currency. Portugal and Greece recorded small increases after 2009 but

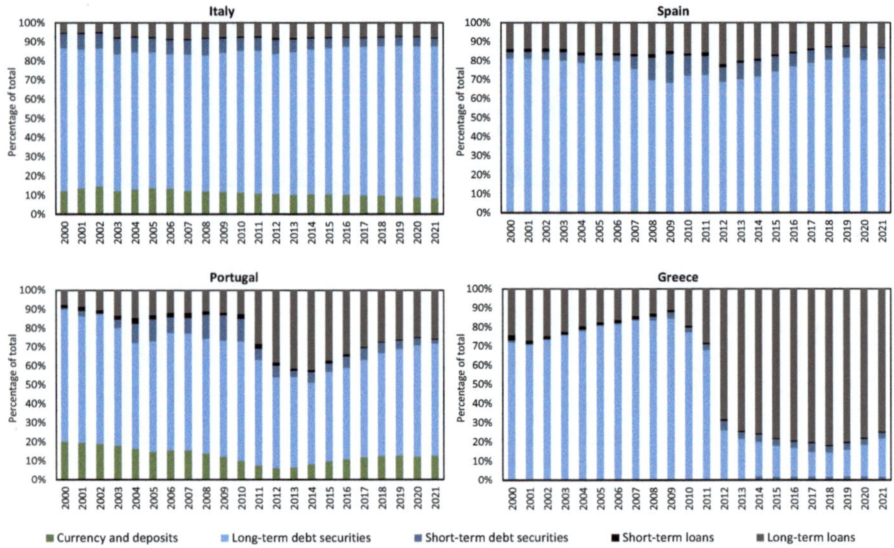

Fig. 7.7 General government gross debt decomposition—financial instruments, shares of total—EU4, 2000–2021. Source: Eurostat (2022a), own calculations and processing

were negligible and later disappeared. As of 2021, the EU4 countries show practically no foreign currency-denominated debts.

Figure 7.7 shows the structure of the debts regarding financial instrument composition. It represents the first step in analysing government financing needs. These findings are crucial for short-term and long-term funding prospects of government liabilities. Italy, Spain, and Portugal have most of their general government debt in long-term debt securities. The ratio is similar to the Euro Area countries. According to Eurostat (2022a), the EU19 countries had more than 85% of their general government debts stored in long-term debt securities as of 2021.

Since 2012, Greece has transformed most of its debt into long-term loans making their financing needs more spread in time, making it easier to repay. A similar occurrence was in Portugal; however, the magnitudes were much lower, and the long-term loan shares have started to decline since 2014.

Table 7.2 shows the residual maturities of government debt securities between 2009 and 2019. The shorter the maturity is, the more liquidity (short-term financial funds) the country needs to have. All the countries' values were rather close to the EU19 aggregate for the examined period with few exceptions. First, the EU19 countries managed to, on (weighted) average, increase their residual maturities from 2009 to 2021 by 1.5 years. Second, Greece had more than average residual maturity for the whole period, which was a positive occurring per se. Finally, Portugal had a comparatively shorter residual maturity. As of 2021, Italy and Portugal are showing below-average values. From this point of view, these countries need more prompt financial resources.

Table 7.2 Average residual maturity of government debt securities (non-consolidated, outstanding amounts) in years—EU4, 2009–2021

Year	EU19 average	Italy	Spain	Portugal	Greece
2009	6.4	7.3	6.5	6.1	7.9
2010	6.4	7.4	6.7	6.1	7.3
2011	6.3	7.2	5.9	6.0	6.8
2012	6.3	6.8	5.7	5.5	7.8
2013	6.3	6.6	5.3	5.1	7.9
2014	6.5	6.5	5.9	5.8	8.5
2015	6.6	6.6	6.2	6.6	8.5
2016	6.9	6.8	6.6	6.4	8.0
2017	7.1	7.0	7.0	6.1	8.3
2018	7.3	6.9	7.4	6.1	7.7
2019	7.5	6.9	7.6	6.3	8.0
2020	7.7	7.0	7.8	6.5	9.2
2021	7.9	7.1	7.8	7.1	9.5

Source: ECB (2022), own processing

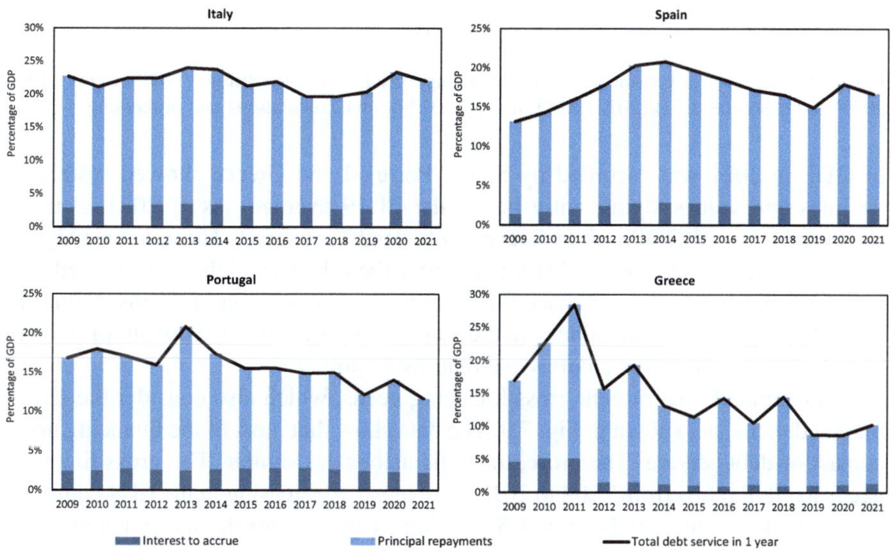

Fig. 7.8 General government debt service (due in 1 year) decomposition, GDP ratios—EU4, 2009–2021. Source: ECB (2022), own calculations and processing

Figure 7.8 shows the structure of the debt service for the EU4 countries. The developments and the size of debt services are vastly different. However, most of the debt service consists of principal repayments. For illustration, the debt service for the EU19 aggregate was 14% of its GDP, and principal repayments contributed by only 1.3 pp. (Eurostat, 2022a). Italy consistently showed the highest values for most of the examined period. In 2019, its debt service level was roughly 22% of its GDP, which may be considered alarming. A lower but still above-average value of 16.7%

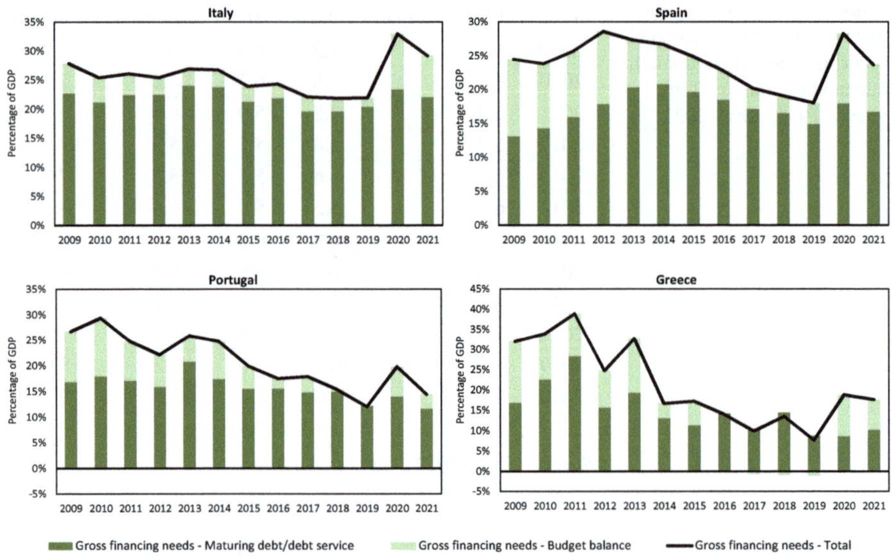

Fig. 7.9 General government gross financing needs decomposition, GDP ratios—EU4, 2009–2021. Source: ECB (2022) and Eurostat (2022a), own calculations and processing

of GDP in 2021 was recorded by Spain. Portugal and Greece showed systematic declines and values significantly below the EU19 average. As of 2021, Portugal showed 11.6% of GDP, while Greece only 10.2% of GDP. These values significantly affected these countries' ability to repay their debts, and they also helped their fiscal policies have a higher space for discretionary policies and reforms. Nevertheless, these systematic declines in the case of Greece were a result of '*rescue programmes*' rather than a purely national fiscal policy.

Total general government gross financing needs, which also consider the size of budget deficits, are shown in Fig. 7.9. The data show that most of the financing needs consist of debt service. Therefore, the conclusions are similar. The gross financing needs to GDP ratios from 2009 to 2019 were mostly decreasing in the EU4 countries. However, the values of Italy and Spain were considerably high compared to the EU19 aggregate, which showed 19.1% of GDP in 2021. The fact indicates significant liquidity pressures.

The levels of private-sector debts also need to be examined. The values are crucial because higher private indebtedness lowers the capacity to fund public debt. According to Eurostat (2022a) and this author's own calculations, the simple average of the consolidated private sector debt to GDP ratios for the EU19 countries was 138.4% in 2020. Italy and Greece recorded below-average values of 118.4% and 125.4% of GDP. At the same time, Spain and Portugal showed significantly higher values of 147.1% and 163.7% of their GDPs.

Finally, it is necessary to consider that changes in the total debt stock usually do not reflect the changes in the overall budget balances perfectly. This is shown in the so-called stock-flow adjustment indicator, which covers transactions that affect the

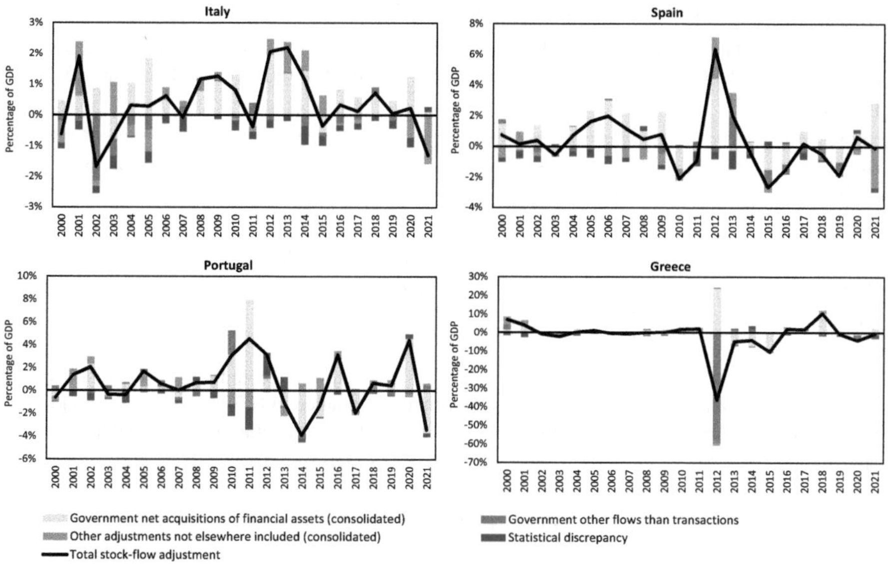

Fig. 7.10 General government debt—stock-flow adjustment decomposition, GDP ratios—EU4, 2000–2021. Source: ECB (2022), own calculations and processing

overall level of debt stock but are not recorded in the budget balances. The transactions may include privatisation receipts, debt relief, bank recapitalisation expenditures, and other factors.

The stock-flow adjustments are usually significant and can be subject to various practices that may show the debt level in a more positive outlook than it deserves. The values for the EU4 countries are shown in Fig. 7.10. Positive values increase the overall debt stock, while negative values decrease the level of debt. First, the values were relatively high in the EU4 countries. Second, the countries showed significant volatility during the financial crisis (2010–2014). Third, Greece recorded a substantial decrease in its debt level in 2012. According to Xafa (2014), it was the largest debt restructuring in the history of sovereign defaults and the first within the Euro Area. The Greek debt relief of 2012 amounted to roughly 60% of its GDP. Nevertheless, it was arguably '*too little too late*' in terms of restoring the debt sustainability of Greece (ibid.).

7.1.3 Selected Benchmarks

Table 7.3 shows selected fiscal benchmarks based on empirical works of international institutions. The European Commission's indicators were obtained from the

Table 7.3 Selected benchmark indicators—EU4, 2021

Country/ benchmark	Gross gen. gov. debt to GDP	Debt share of non-residents	Private sector debt to GDP	Short-term gov. debt share (Δ)
Benchmark —EC	60%	–	133%	–
Benchmark —IMF	60% to 70%	30% to 45%	–	+1.5 pp to +2 pp
Italy	150.8%	29.2%	118.4%[a]	−1.1 pp
Spain	118.4%	42.8%	138.1%	−0.6 pp
Portugal	127.4%	45.2%	157.6%	−1.2 pp
Greece	193.3%	N/A	121.0%	−0.3 pp

Country/ benchmark	Gov. gross financing needs to GDP	Bond spread vs. Germany (bps)[b]	Current account balance to GDP (3-year average)	Net investment position to GDP
Benchmark —EC	–	–	+6% to −4%	−35%
Benchmark —IMF	15% to 20%	+400 to +600 bps	+5% to −5%	–
Italy	29.2%	143 bps	3.4%	+8.1%
Spain	23.6%	79 bps	1.2%	−71.5%
Portugal	14.5%	74 bps	−0.6%	−94.7%
Greece	17.6%	167 bps	−4.9%	−170.8%

Source: ECB (2022) and Eurostat (2022a), own calculations and processing
[a]Value for 2020 was used due to data unavailability
[b]Long-term government bond yields are used (≈10-year maturity, EMU converg. criterion)

Macroeconomic Imbalance Procedure Scoreboard (Eurostat, 2022b) and the IMF's benchmarks from their relevant fiscal guidelines[4] (see IMF, 2013). It shows the values as of 2021 when the countries are slowly recovering from the COVID-19 crisis.

The situation of the EU4 countries is alarming. As of 2021, there is no clear outlier. The conclusions are dependent on the chosen indicator. However, Italy and Greece show the largest interest rate spreads against Germany. The indicator shows the overall risk perception of investors.

[4]The IMF provides a broad spectrum of possible benchmark values. Therefore, the table uses intervals that are denoting either medium- or high-risk values.

7.2 Fiscal Stances, Fiscal Efforts, and Related Indicators

The character of government fiscal policies is evaluated by budget balance measures. The overall budget balance (OB) is defined as the difference between government revenue (R) and expenditure (G). Considering nominal GDP (Y) ratios, the following expression is obtained:

$$\frac{\mathrm{OB}_t}{Y_t} = \frac{R_t - G_t}{Y_t}.$$

Nonetheless, the directly observable fiscal measures are influenced by various factors. As a result, it is not possible to interpret them properly when examining government fiscal efforts. The problem can be illustrated by two cases when the state of the economy is not in equilibrium—when the actual output does not equal potential output.[5]

Let the individual fiscal items be denoted by * when they refer to the potential levels of the variables. Equation below depicts when the economy is in its expansionary phase of a business cycle.[6] In this case, the actual government revenue is higher than the potential government revenue. At the same time, the actual government expenditure is lower than its potential level:

$$Y > Y^* \rightarrow \frac{R}{Y} > \frac{R^*}{Y^*} \wedge \frac{G}{Y} \leq \frac{G^*}{Y^*},$$

→ Overall budget balance > Cyclically-adjusted budget balance.

As a result, the overall budget balance is higher than the cyclically-adjusted measure. In other words, the fiscal situation is looking better than it actually is. The public may mistakenly compliment the government for its consolidation efforts when, in fact, the budget balance was significantly influenced by economic expansion.

The opposite case, when the economy is in recession, is depicted in the following equation:

$$Y < Y^* \rightarrow \frac{R}{Y} < \frac{R^*}{Y^*} \wedge \frac{G}{Y} \geq \frac{G^*}{Y^*},$$

→ Overall budget balance < Cyclically-adjusted budget balance.

The estimation of various factors, which affect the overall budget balances, needs to be examined because it can significantly influence the interpretation of

[5]Due to simplicity, we abstract from other factors and focus on business cycle effects that are dominant.

[6]There can be situations when the assumptions about government expenditure do not hold. However, such situations are rare.

government efforts. Therefore, the next subchapters discuss these characteristics and related issues.

7.2.1 Estimation of Structural Budget Balances

The principle behind obtaining a structural budget balance is to adjust the overall balance for effects that cannot be interpreted as a result of a systematic government effort. A widely accepted practice is to adjust the overall budget balance for business cycle effects (*cyclically-adjusted balance*[7]) and one-off transactions and other temporary measures (*structural budget balance*).[8] It should be noted that some institutions[9] adjust the overall balance also for effects other than business cycle fluctuations. However, they are not used in the presented estimations. I discuss the rationale in the relevant section below. The used definition is depicted in the following equation (Kremer et al., 2006, p. 9):

$$X_s = X - X_c - X_m \ ,$$

where:

X_s is the structural indicator.
X is the unadjusted indicator.
X_c is the cyclical component (business cycle effects).
X_m is the size of one-off and other temporary measures.

The previous equation does not explicitly state the methods used and the order of the adjustment steps, which is crucial. In particular, the size of one-off and other temporary measures needs to be deducted from the budget balance before a cyclical adjustment is made to avoid biased estimates.[10] The applied procedure is summarised in Fig. 7.11.

The cyclically-adjusted budget balance (CAOB) works with potential levels of the variables and is defined as follows (see Bornhorst et al., 2011):

[7] The cyclically-adjusted budget balance is sometimes incorrectly referred to as the structural budget balance. The latter excludes effects of one-off and other temporary measures, in addition to the cyclical adjustment.

[8] Alternatively, one may also subtract the effects of interest payments and work with primary budget balances.

[9] For example, the IMF.

[10] If the cyclical adjustment were applied first, the one-off and other temporary measures would be considered during the process.

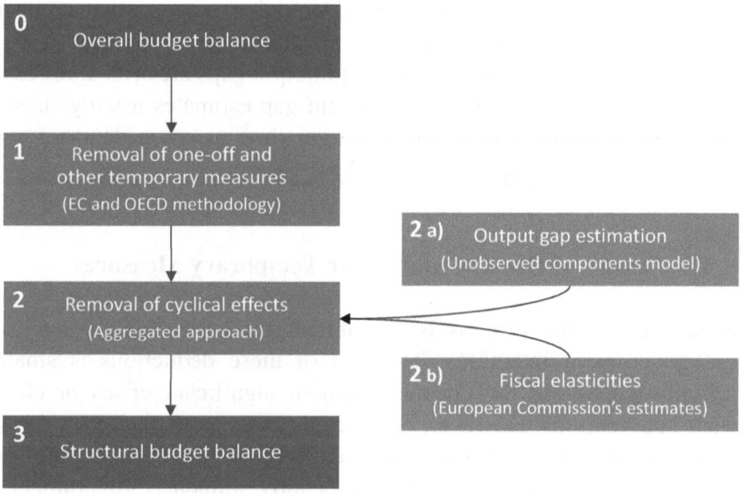

Fig. 7.11 Structural budget balance estimation procedure. Source: Own processing

$$\mathrm{CAOB} = \frac{\mathrm{OB}^*}{Y^*} = \frac{R^*}{Y^*} - \frac{G^*}{Y^*} = \frac{R}{Y^*}\left(\frac{R^*}{R}\right) - \frac{G}{Y^*}\left(\frac{G^*}{G}\right).$$

Considering constant revenue elasticity (η_{R}), constant expenditure elasticity (η_{G}), solving differential equations of order one, and multiplying each equation by the individual budget item, gives the definitions of cyclically adjusted budget components:

$$R\left(\frac{R^*}{R}\right) = R\left(\frac{Y^*}{Y}\right)^{\eta_{\mathrm{R}}},$$

$$G\left(\frac{G^*}{G}\right) = G\left(\frac{Y^*}{Y}\right)^{\eta_{\mathrm{G}}}.$$

The values of fiscal elasticities[11] are assumptions regarding the size of business cycle effects in the budget balances. They refer to the percentage change in one variable (budget item) to a one-percentage-point change in another variable (output gap). I follow the European Commission's methodology and use the aggregated approach, which means using the output gap as a single measure of the business cycle, applied to all fiscal items (see Mourre et al., 2019). Furthermore, factors other

[11] The European Commission is also working with fiscal semi-elasticities that are defined as the elasticities of GDP ratios of relevant budget items to output gap. The cyclically adjusted budget balance can be approximated using the overall budget semi-elasticity. The European Commission is using this simplified definition when informing policymakers. See Mourre et al. (2014, p. 9).

than the business cycle effects[12] are not considered due to appropriate comparability of the estimated measures among the examined countries.

Finally, the values of one-off measures and output gaps are critical for estimating structural budget balances. In particular, output gap estimates usually substantially differ across international institutions and over time as more data are available. Hence, the following subchapter analyses these issues.

7.2.1.1 The Nature of One-Off and Other Temporary Measures

An essential step of the process is to subtract measures that do not represent systematic government intentions. The size of these deductions is small under normal circumstances—in the episodes without significant crises or changes in government interventions. However, one-off measures were one of the tools of the so-called creative accounting[13] in the past (see Koen & Noord, 2005). Although the measures are non-recurrent, they can significantly influence government budget balances. Therefore, the measures need to be closely examined.

There are no universally accepted criteria for identifying one-off or temporary fiscal measures. Hence, the procedure requires considerable judgement (see Bornhorst et al., 2011). I decided to use the European Commission's estimates because of direct comparability. However, the Commission's (2022a) AMECO database does not provide historical values before 2010 for three of the four countries—Spain, Portugal, and Greece. I obtained these estimates from the OECD's Economic Outlook database (OECD, 2022). The differences between the European Commission's and the OECD's estimates after 2010 are relatively small regarding the three mentioned countries.

The size of one-off and other temporary measures used in the subsequent calculation is shown in Fig. 7.12 and compared to the actual budget balances of the EU4 countries. The values are insignificant except for specific data points that need to be explained. The one-offs of Italy contributed to a lower (worse) structural budget balance compared to the actual balance between 2000 and 2005. The Italian government benefited from one-off real estate sales, tax amnesty revenues, and one-off tax revenues, which should not be included in the structural budget balances (IMF, 2005). The structural budget balance of the country does not significantly benefit from one-off measures conducted during the outbreak of the financial crisis, which contrasts with the other examined countries. This fact needs to be considered in the structural budget analysis.

Spain, Portugal, and Greece showed a significant positive impact of the measures on the structural budget balances between 2010 and 2017. Most of the non-recurrent transactions were realised because of the effects of the 2008–2009 financial crisis.

[12] These factors might include asset prices, commodity prices, terms of trade, or output composition effects (see Bornhorst et al., 2011).

[13] The term refers to malpractices used for improving basic fiscal and economic indicators.

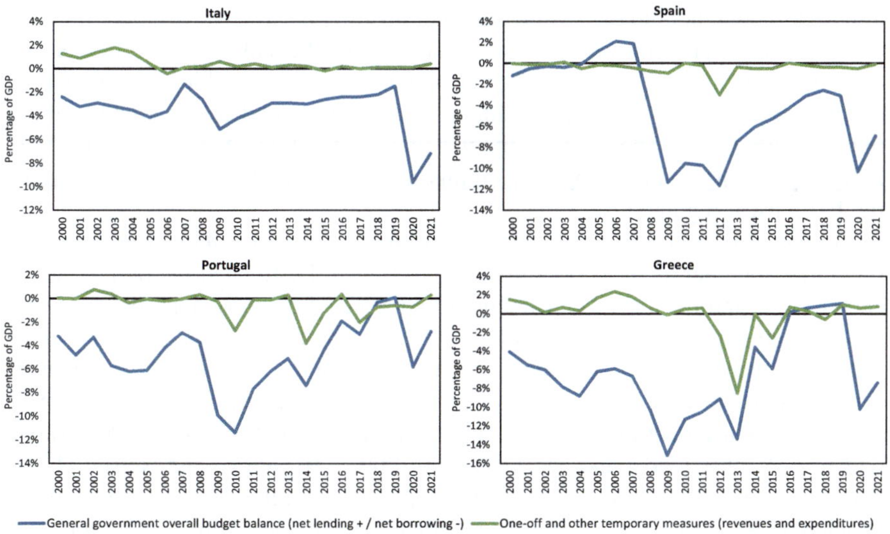

Fig. 7.12 Size of one-off and other temporary measures and actual budget balances—EU4, 2000–2021. Note: A minus sign means a positive effect on the adjusted budget balance measure. It indicates a lower deficit or a higher surplus. Source: European Commission (2022a), Eurostat (2022a), and OECD (2022), own calculations and processing

The 2012 one-off measures of Spain mostly consisted of expenditures used for bank recapitalisation (OECD, 2012). The measures of Portugal consisted of one-off bank recapitalisation expenditure and pension fund transfers (IMF, 2016). Finally, measures of Greece consisted of a broad range of one-off and other ad-hoc adjustments, including bank recapitalisation expenditure (IMF, 2017).

7.2.1.2 Estimation of Output Gaps and Their Pitfalls

The most critical component of a structural budget balance is the estimation of business-cycle effects, which is determined by output gap and potential GDP estimates. A positive value indicates economic expansion, while a negative value indicates an economic recession. The output gap (Y^{GAP}) is the difference between actual GDP (Y) and potential GDP (Y^*):

$$Y^{GAP} = \frac{(Y - Y^*)}{Y^*} \quad .$$

It is possible to simply take and analyse the estimates of international institutions such as the European Commission, IMF, or OECD. Nevertheless, the approach is not advisable due to a variety of reasons. First, there is no unified methodology on how the estimates should be made. The output gap is an unobserved variable, and the outcomes significantly differ depending on the estimation method used. Second, although the methodologies of international institutions are very detailed, the institutions may suffer from serious biases, including conflicts of interest.[14] In this case, their interpretation of the events would be taken implicitly. Third, the output gap estimates of the European Commission might have been underestimating the amplitude of output gaps. The EU4 countries belong in the Euro Area. Hence, the book focuses primarily on the European Commission's estimates because these are used in the EU's fiscal regulations.

Output gaps can be estimated through various methods, and there is no consensus on which approach is the most suitable one. Hence, I estimated the output gap for each EU4 country using various methods and selected the most appropriate method based on good judgement. The methods used consist of three main types: traditional filtration techniques, unorthodox techniques, and unobserved components (UC) models. In addition, I employ commonly used parameters in the literature. The methods used are based on the works of Hodrick and Prescott (1997), Baxter and King (1999), Christiano and Fitzgerald (2003), Beveridge and Nelson (1981), Kamber et al. (2018), Kožić and Sever (2014), Hamilton (2018), Percival and Walden (2008), and the unobserved components models utilise the models of Grant and Chan (2017a, 2017b, 2017c).

The models are estimated using the longest available time-series data. The univariate approaches work with real quarterly GDP data starting from 1960. Moreover, the multivariate estimates incorporate general unemployment rate and consumer price index (CPI) data. The length of the used time series of the unemployment rate and inflation rate is relatively shorter; the starting year ranges from 1983 to 1990. The length is dependent on the particular time series and country. All the variables are seasonally adjusted.

Figure 7.13 presents 11 different model estimates of output gaps for each country between 2000 and 2019. According to the previous analyses, the EU4 economies were significantly overheated before the primary effects of the 2008–2009 financial crisis occurred. Later, however, the countries were running far below their potential level. The situation began to change between 2014 and 2015, except for Greece, which was still running below its potential GDP level. After 2020, the countries showed another significant fall below their potential GDP levels due to the coronavirus crisis. Nevertheless, the declines for Greece and Portugal were of a smaller magnitude than during the previous. Only Italy showed a likely more significant drop than during the previous financial crisis, as the country was hit by the COVID-19 crisis significantly in 2020.

According to the estimates, Greece likely experienced the largest shocks to the output gap dynamics. The second largest output gap dynamics was in Spain,

[14] For example, the European Commission uses the estimates when evaluating fiscal compliance in the EU according to the Medium-Term Budgetary Objectives within the Stability and Growth Pact. In addition, the IMF also participated in addressing fiscal issues in the past. It was lending money to Greece as a response to the effects of the 2008–2009 financial crisis. It should also be noted that a delegation of certain powers to a decentralised unit does not solve the issue since the agent is financed by the principal.

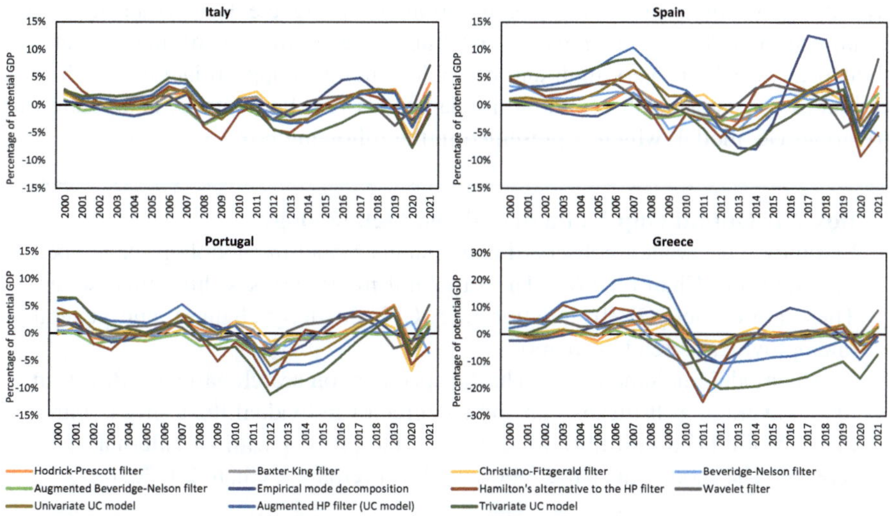

Fig. 7.13 Various output gap estimates—EU4, 2000–2021. Note: Specifications of the methods used are provided in the text. The figure purposely uses the same scale, except for Greece, which is an outlier, to compare the magnitudes of the output gap dynamics. Source: Own calculations and processing

followed by Portugal and Italy. Moreover, a plausible benchmark in evaluating the estimates is inflation rate development. According to Buti et al. (2019), there is a significant correlation between the output gap and inflation.[15] Sample standard deviations of the corresponding HICPs between 2007 and 2021 confirm the country order. Greece showed the highest value, followed by Spain, Portugal, and Italy (Eurostat, 2022a).

The decision of which method produces the most favourable results is not straightforward. However, traditional filtering techniques, such as the HP filter, suffer from serious biases. Possibly the two most important facts are their inability to separate trend from cycle in the case of significant shocks—economic instabilities[16] and end-point bias.

Both traditional and unorthodox techniques did not produce plausible results when contrasted with theoretical and empirical knowledge of the output gap dynamics and the estimates of international institutions. Thus, I focus on the models of unobserved components. The presented univariate UC model shows rather low

[15]However, the authors mention that a one-to-one relationship between the inflation rate and the output gap should not be expected. The issue is more complicated as inflation is not only driven by demand pressure but also by external supply shocks (for example, low raw material and oil price inflation), which are not directly influenced by output gap dynamics.

[16]For example, significant instability may be depicted by a double-dip recession which was experienced by Italy, Spain, and Portugal in the selected period. Greece experienced one but significantly larger shock, which may distort the estimates.

dynamics, which is not a valid assumption regarding the EU4 countries in the examined period. The augmented HP filter gives estimates of the output gap dynamics, which are very high and unstable. The most appropriate model, having estimates consistent with economic fundamentals for all countries, is arguably the trivariate UC model, which is presented in the following box.

Box 7.1 Output Gap Estimates—Used Methodology

I employ a trivariate unobserved components model methodology developed by Grant and Chan (2017c). The structural model utilises three time series. These are output (GDP), inflation rate (CPI, quarterly change), and general unemployment rate (15+ years).

The model implements a stochastic specification search based on Bayesian model averaging. It means that some degree of individual flexibility is introduced while keeping full transparency of the process without external interference. The model takes the following form (Grant & Chan, 2017c, p. 5):

$$\pi_t - \pi_t^* = \rho^\pi (\pi_{t-1} - \pi_{t-1}^*) + \delta_{\lambda^u} \lambda^u (u_t - u_t^*) + \delta_{\lambda y} \lambda^y (y_t - y_t^*) + \varepsilon_t^\pi,$$

$$y_t - y_t^* = \delta_{\gamma^u} \gamma^u (u_t - u_t^*) + c_t,$$

$$u_t - u_t^* = \rho_1^u (u_{t-1} - u_{t-1}^*) + \rho_2^u (u_{t-2} - u_{t-2}^*) + \varepsilon_t^u,$$

$$c_t = \rho_1^c c_{t-1} + \rho_2^c c_{t-2} + \varepsilon_t^c,$$

where:

- y_t is output measure, y_t^* is potential output.
- π_t is inflation rate, π_t^* is natural rate of inflation.
- u_t is unemployment rate.
- u_t^* is the non-accelerating inflation rate of unemployment (NAIRU).
- ρ is autoregressive component.
- c_t is cyclical component of output.
- δ is binary (dummy) variable used for stochastic specification search.
- ε is independent innovation (error term).

The inflation gap in the first equation states that the deviation of inflation from its underlying trend depends on both the unemployment gap and the output gap. When inflation and output are at trend levels, inflation equals its underlying trend plus a transitory AR(1) component. The second equation relates the output gap to the unemployment gap where γ^u is Okun's coefficient. Finally, the third equation represents the unemployment gap, and the last equation describes the cyclical component of output, while both are assumed to follow a stationary AR(2) process. More detailed information about the methodology used is available in the work of Grant and Chan (2017c).

Another important dimension of the analysis is a comparison with the estimates of international institutions. The European Commission, OECD, and IMF regularly estimate the output gaps. The mentioned institutions use a production function approach,[17] where the potential output is a function of trend capital, labour, and total factor productivity. The main differences lie in the determination of trend unemployment. The European Commission is calculating its estimates based on the non-accelerating wage rate of unemployment—NAWRU (Mourre et al., 2014).

In contrast, the OECD is using a non-accelerating inflation rate of unemployment—NAIRU (Chalaux & Guillemette, 2019). The IMF methodology differs from country to country, but a production function approach predominates for advanced economies (Bornhorst et al., 2011). Furthermore, the OECD and the IMF allow for more judgement in shaping the officially reported output gaps (Hristov et al., 2017). The approach produces less comparable estimates among the examined countries. There is a trade-off between international comparability and flexibility. The main argument for international comparability in our case is that the European Commission is using its estimates in fiscal policy monitoring, which is connected to the fiscal regulations in the EU.[18] As it was mentioned, there is no solid evidence to see the estimates of these institutions as superior to other estimates for various reasons. The two most prominent reasons are potential conflicts of interest and methodological biases.

The European Commission has been facing intense criticism from international experts regarding their output gap estimations. According to the EU Independent Fiscal Institutions Network (2018), the estimates may be influenced by technical parameters such as the Cobb–Douglas' alpha coefficient, the choice of Bayesian priors, post-estimation adjustments, or other factors. The criticism led the authors of the European Commission's methodology to revise it. In an unofficial statement, they claimed that an element of flexibility and judgement had been introduced into the fiscal surveillance process to deal with specific circumstances (see Buti et al., 2019). These include situations where the potential output estimates depart from plausible estimates based on other cyclical indicators. In addition, a range of country-specific changes have been approved (ibid.). However, these model adjustments were implemented primarily due to the initiative of individual EU Member States (EUIFIN, 2018). It indicates that technical details have significantly influenced fiscal policy decisions in the EU in recent years. Consequently, seemingly innocent technical assumptions have become objects of political demands (EUIFIN, 2018).

A comparison of output gap estimates of the trivariate UC model and the selected international institutions is depicted in Fig. 7.14. The estimates of the European

[17]The approach is rather a (dis)aggregation method. The approaches to the estimation of the individual components drive the final estimates.

[18]For example, I refer to the Excessive Deficit Procedure (EDP) or the Macroeconomic Imbalance Procedure (MIP). More broadly, the regulations are set in the Stability and Growth Pact and the so-called European Fiscal Compact.

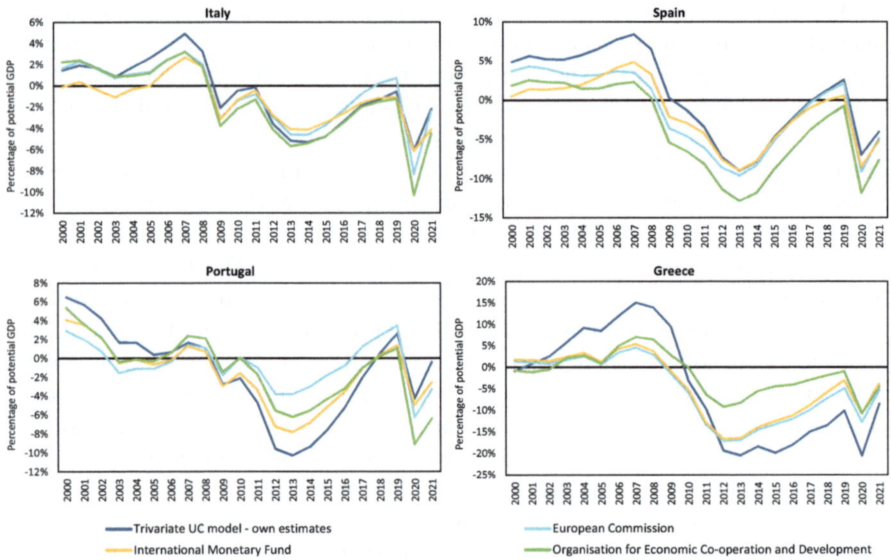

Fig. 7.14 Comparison of contemporaneous output gap estimates—EU4, 2000–2021. Source: European Commission (2022a), IMF (2022), OECD (2022), own calculations and processing

Commission are arguably not consistent. They seem to underestimate the magnitude of the output gaps when compared to the other model estimates in the case of Italy and Portugal between 2012 and 2019. The Italian Minister of Economy and Finance, Roberto Gualtieri, recently stressed the issue and sent a letter to the European Commission's officials in October 2019 regarding the problem (Gualtieri, 2019). The possible bias is noticeable in the magnitudes of output gaps of the EU4 before the financial crisis. The EU's fiscal regulation was inadequately loose before the financial crisis.[19] The COVID-19 crisis was specific due to the lockdowns; however, the problem was also present.[20]

The EU4 countries were gradually overheating due to expansive economic policies and low interest rates in the Euro Area before 2008. For example, Greece's final consumption expenditure to GDP ratio was more than 90% in 2009, by far the largest in the EU (Eurostat, 2022a). At the same time, the European Commission's estimates show that these countries were '*overheated*' by approximately 2.5–5% above potential GDP at their peaks. For illustration, the weighted average (aggregate indicator) for the EU27 showed a positive gap of 2.9% in 2007 (European Commission, 2022a). The European Commission's estimates assume that countries like the Czech Republic, Slovakia, or Latvia were overheating much more significantly than

[19] It refers to the relation of the structural budget balances to the Medium-Term Budgetary Framework implemented in the Stability and Growth Pact.

[20] Nonetheless, the EU4 countries were likely experiencing negative output gaps. Hence, the issue was possibly less significant.

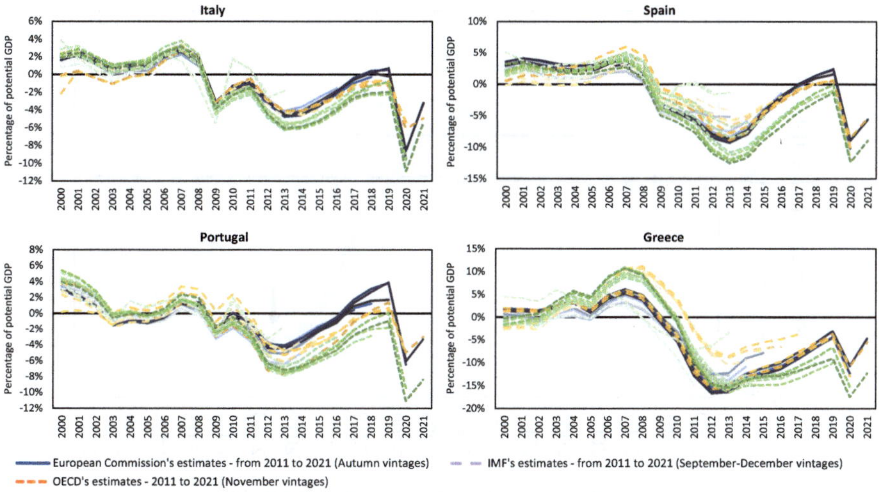

Fig. 7.15 Comparison of historical output gap estimates—EU4, 2000–2021 (late 2011–2021 vintages). Note: The figure uses data vintages starting from 2011 because the prior estimates are not available in the European Commission's AMECO database. Source: European Commission (2022a), IMF (2022), OECD (2022), own processing

the EU4 countries.[21] The estimated value of Greece was 4.5%, while the Czech Republic showed 5.8%, Slovakia 5.9%, and Latvia even 11.3% in 2007 (ibid.).

Further evidence of the possible systematic bias of the European Commission's estimates is shown in Fig. 7.15. It depicts different estimate vintages of the selected international institutions between 2011 and 2021. The European Commission's estimates were of a significantly lower magnitude between 2006 and 2010 for Portugal, Spain, and Greece. Furthermore, it should also be noted that the IMF drastically changed its estimates for Greece in 2018, making them identical to those of the European Commission. Since 2018, these two institutions have been providing nearly identical estimates.[22] In other words, there is an apparent synchronisation, possibly due to the common lending programmes and monitoring. In the past, the IMF estimated much larger overheating of the Greek economy, which is in accordance with the presented argumentation and is arguably closer to reality. The differences between late 2017 and 2018 vintages are shown in Fig. 7.16. The OECD did not significantly change its estimates during the examined period.

Furthermore, it is necessary to mention that, according to my estimates, Greece showed the highest overheating prior to 2009 out of the four examined countries. The estimates of Spain (3.5%) and Italy (3.2%) were near the EU average, while the estimate of Portugal (1.4%) was below the average (Eurostat, 2022a). I do not find

[21] In total, the European Commission output gap estimates assume that ten EU countries were overheating more significantly than Greece (European Commission, 2022a).

[22] Including the coronavirus crisis episode.

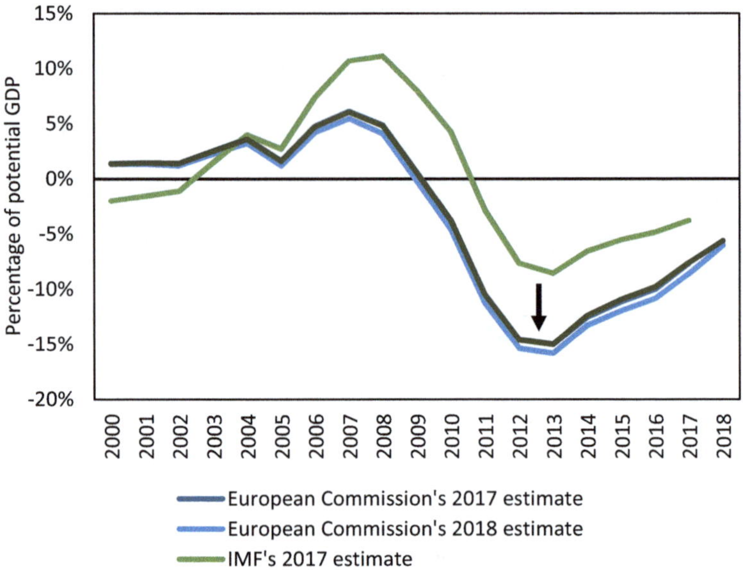

Fig. 7.16 Comparison of historical output gap estimates—Greece, 2000–2018 (late 2017 and 2018 vintages). Source: European Commission (2022a) and IMF (2022), own processing

the results to be consistent and economically plausible. The trivariate UC model estimates suggest that the overheating episodes of the EU4 countries, and the overall output gap dynamics, were of a higher magnitude than assumed by the European Commission. The advantage of the used model is its direct comparability among the countries, transparency, and flexibility due to the use of stochastic specification search.

The COVID-19 pandemic and the associated lockdowns and restrictive measures led to another significant decline in output gaps of the EU4 countries. However, the effects significantly differed among the EU4 countries. For instance, Italy showed a larger negative output gap than during the previous financial crisis, while the other countries showed similar or even less pronounced declines—depending on the estimates used.

7.2.2 *Development of Estimated Indicators*

The final results of the previous calculations are presented and analysed in this section. Figure 7.17 compares the estimates of structural budget balances with those of the European Commission.[23] The differences are notable in the case of all four

[23] The differences are strictly driven by the different estimations of output gaps.

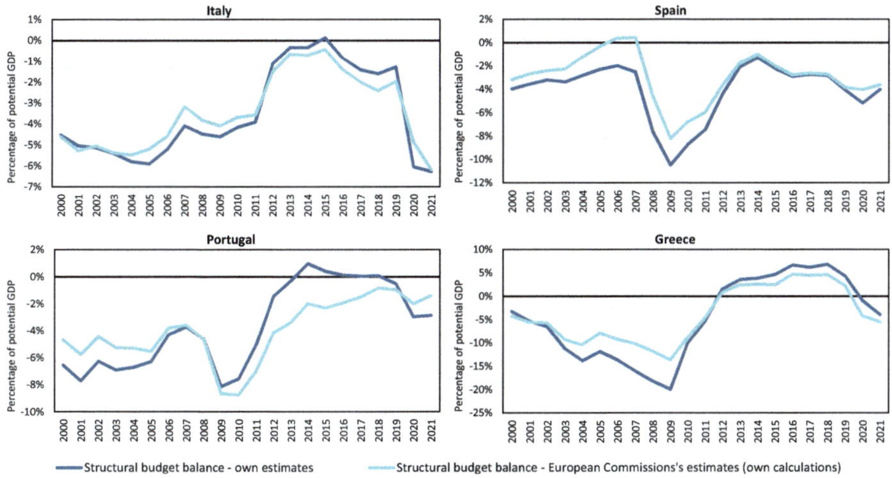

Fig. 7.17 Comparison of structural budget balance estimates with the European Commission's estimates—EU4, 2000–2021. Note: The European Commission estimates are calculated using the parameters that they currently use. However, they utilise some estimates of one-off measures published by the OECD before 2010. The European Commission does not publish estimates prior to 2010. Source: European Commission (2022a) and OECD (2022), own calculations and processing

examined countries. The own estimations suggest that the fiscal performance of the countries before the financial crisis of 2008–2009 was much worse. Later, the estimates are closer to the European Commission's values. The exception is Portugal after 2009, where a better performance was estimated—it meant a sharper fiscal consolidation effort than the European Commission assumed.

Figure 7.18 compares the structural indicators with overall budget balances. The data show that the two measures differ significantly, and three main periods can be identified. First, until 2007–2011, the fiscal policy stances or discretionary fiscal policies were much more expansionary than suggested by the overall balances. The situation was caused by prohibitive motivations (moral hazard) as well as inefficient regulations and over-optimism, which is typical for a period of relatively strong economic growth.[24] Second, the data show episodes of significant fiscal consolidation efforts after 2009, pronounced especially in Greece. It was caused by several factors. Strong political demand and the initiation of '*rescue programmes*'[25] favoured fiscal austerity.

Moreover, the ECB initiated its quantitative easing programme. Its first round was in effect from 2010 to 2012. It was reinitiated later for its second and third

[24] However, note that the EU4 countries were not necessarily doing well in this regard. The whole EU provided external demand and incentives for the examined countries.

[25] I use quotes because these programmes did not serve the rescue purpose. They were designed to mitigate the worst political and economic consequences in the short and medium term for the Euro Area. They did not solve anything. The same argument can be made for monetary policy decisions.

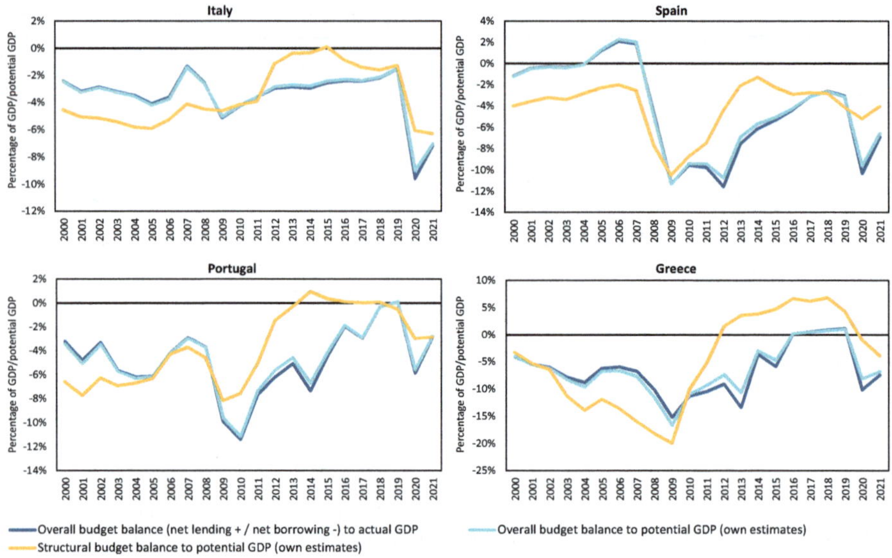

Fig. 7.18 Comparison between overall budget balances and structural budget balances—EU4, 2000–2021. Source: Eurostat (2022a), own calculations and processing

phases in 2014 and 2019, respectively. The ECB reached zero lower bound with its interest rates, provided vast amounts of liquidity to the banking system, and partly restored confidence in the markets. It is difficult to argue that the intervention was inappropriate during the recession. However, this institution continued with the policy even after the worst effects were mitigated. One of the possible reasons was intense political pressure. It resulted in a continuous and strong incentive for moral hazard or socialisation of risks, which has enabled the EU4 countries to continue with unsustainable policies without significant structural reforms for which the monetary policy is no substitute.[26] Until 2020, the countries experienced economic growth again after the worst effects of the crisis had been mitigated. Apart from the effects of myopic macroeconomic policies, one of the reasons was a recovery of external demand. It helped the countries achieve better fiscal results because of higher government revenues and a higher comparative base.[27] Finally, the COVID-19 crisis showed another significant decline in the balances and further expansionary fiscal stimulations. However, some of the countries showed this tendency even before the crisis.

[26] In the most general sense, I refer to reforms that promote economic growth and efficiency. Arguably, the most significant reform for the countries would be an exit from the Euro Area, which would enable currency depreciation and boost economic recovery through the proper functioning of transmission channels.

[27] The fiscal measures are usually expressed as GDP ratios. When the GDP in the denominator rises, the fraction value becomes lower, therefore showing better results.

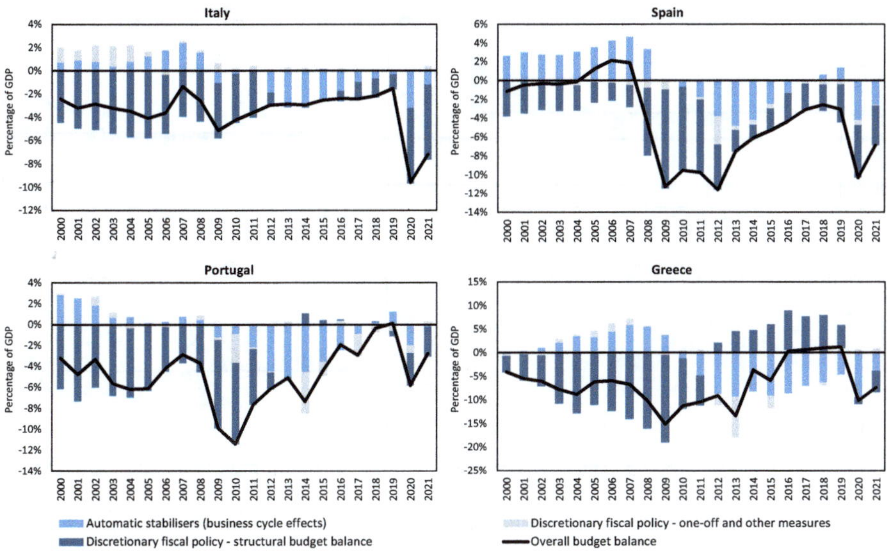

Fig. 7.19 Decomposition of overall budget balances (own estimates)—EU4, 2000–2021. Source: Eurostat (2022a), own calculations and processing

Furthermore, the overall budget balances can be decomposed into fiscal policy elements with direct economic interpretation. A discretionary fiscal policy is represented by one-off measures and structural budget balances. Moreover, under the assumption of no other effects, I separate automatic fiscal stabilisers or business cycle effects. The decomposition is depicted in Fig. 7.19, and two main conclusions can be made.

First, the discretionary fiscal policies dominated most of the examined period for all the countries. The expansionary fiscal efforts were so strong that they fully offset the effects of automatic stabilisers. Second, automatic stabilisers were significant throughout the whole period but became stronger after 2011, except for Spain.

In addition, we need to examine two additional measures for a precise analytical view. The fiscal stance (FS) is defined as the inverse of structural budget balance (BB^{STR}):

$$FS_t = -BB_t^{STR}.$$

Positive values mean an expansionary fiscal stance, while negative values stand for a contractionary fiscal stance. It is often useful to compare this measure to the output gap to assess not only the size of a fiscal stimulus but also its relation to the business cycle. Fiscal policy is one of the two key stabilisation macroeconomic

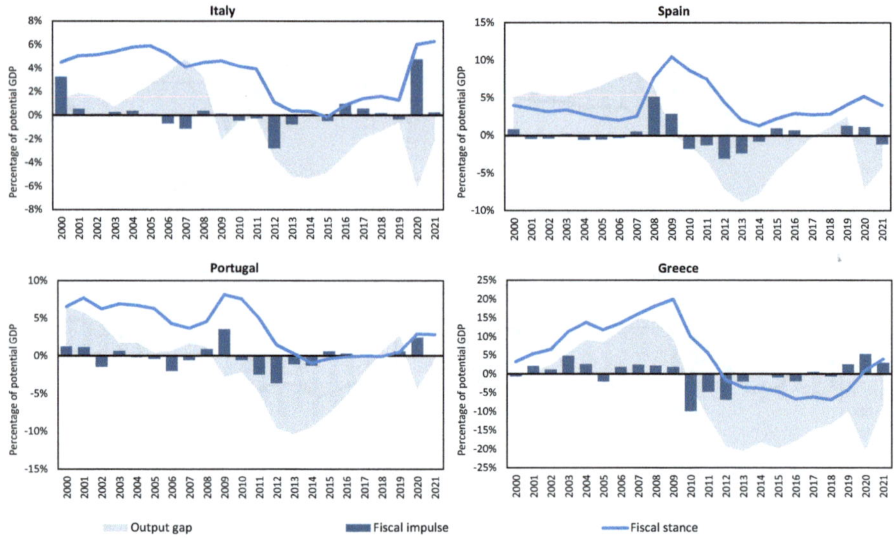

Fig. 7.20 Development of estimated fiscal stances, fiscal impulses, and output gaps—EU4, 2000–2021. Source: Own calculations and processing

policies. Thus, it should aim to be anti-cyclical. Nevertheless, due to various reasons,[28] fiscal policy is often pro-cyclical, destabilising the particular economy.

The fiscal stances of the EU4 countries are shown in Fig. 7.20. The values offer various implications. First, the countries were running structural budget deficits for most of the examined period, thus artificially stimulating the economies. The size of the stimulus peaked for all the countries except Italy.[29] The highest value was recorded in Greece, accounting for nearly 20% of its potential GDP in 2009. The second highest stimulus was made in Spain, reaching approximately 10% of its potential GDP in 2009. These values were extremely high. They even outmatched the size of the GDP gaps at their peaks before the financial crisis of 2008–2009. Although the values were relatively lower in Portugal and Italy, they were still dominant. Hence, I conclude that the fiscal policies caused significant economic instabilities in the countries.

Second, I conclude that pro-cyclical fiscal policies were made before the financial crisis in all the EU4 countries. After 2012, the nature of the policies was less clear;[30] it was either acyclical or anti-cyclical. However, arguably, the latter resulted from the continuation of chronic fiscal deficits rather than systematic fiscal consolidation. Furthermore, Greece is a textbook example of pro-cyclical fiscal policies that amplify the existing output gap and destabilise its economy. The character of fiscal

[28] For example, these include deficit bias, moral hazard, or political budget cycles.

[29] Nevertheless, Italy kept its fiscal stance considerably expansionary for most of the period before the financial crisis.

[30] Note that the estimates suffer from some degree of uncertainty.

policies in Greece, partly due to the design of the '*rescue packages*' is unfortunate. Fiscal rules embedded in the Stability and Growth Pact or in the European Fiscal Compact cannot solve the issues. Paradoxically, they make the problem even worse as they promote policies, which under certain situations—including this one, promote economic instabilities. They are a result of compromises in EU policymaking. They cannot solve the countries' structural problems, which is also the case for monetary policy and quantitative easing in particular. It is evident that the primary purpose is political, not economic. More focus should be put on structural reforms promoting competitiveness and efficiency. This issue is explained in the ninth chapter.

Furthermore, a fiscal impulse[31] (FI) is defined as the first differences or absolute changes of the fiscal stance measure (FS):

$$FI_t = FS_t - FS_{t-1} \ .$$

The interpretation of the measure is the same as in the case of fiscal stance. However, it captures the changes in fiscal stimulus more clearly. The fiscal impulses of the EU4 countries are depicted in Fig. 7.20. The data show that the pro-cyclical nature of fiscal policy in Greece is even more pronounced by using this measure. In addition, the same tendency was in Spain. Finally, I observed serious expansionary fiscal pressure in Portugal and Spain between 2008 and 2009. Contractionary efforts later offset the impulse because it was not sustainable. Moreover, Italy showed a record-high fiscal impulse in 2020 as a reaction to the coronavirus crisis. The impulse was much larger than in the other examined countries.

To sum up, one of the lessons is that strong fiscal efforts are inefficient and destabilising the economy later if a crisis is caused or accompanied by serious structural inefficiencies in the countries.

7.3 Debt Dynamics and Sustainability

The concept of sustainability can be defined from various standpoints. In a nutshell, a sovereign debt sustainability assessment is an informed judgement on a country's capacity to generate and sustain the primary balances required to stabilise or lower the public debt under a large set of circumstances (Debrun et al., 2018).

This section focuses on the most used (traditional) approach to debt sustainability, based on the analysis of debt dynamics (snowball effect). In addition, I present deterministic long-term economic projections based on historical averages of relevant variables between 2000 and 2021. I do not perform a medium-term (stochastic)

[31] The measure has been used by the IMF since the 1970s. Refer to Blejer and Cheasty (1993). Alternative measures with a broader interpretation are various types of fiscal multipliers. This analysis is done in its respective chapter regarding fiscal efficiency.

analysis because the aim is to identify and analyse long-run fiscal patterns and not possible short- to mid-term fluctuations.[32]

Finally, I decided not to include a significant long-term phenomenon of population ageing due to the complications related to incorporating an additional set of assumptions, which is associated with a high degree of uncertainty. The assumptions regarding the relevant economic policies and variables are also frequently revised by the European Commission itself.[33] Hence, the reader should keep in mind that population ageing will put additional pressure on the EU government budget balances in the future.

Box 7.2 Debt Dynamics and Sustainability—Analytical Framework

The debt dynamics analysis is based on the works of the IMF.[34] I assume that the government can borrow debt both from abroad and domestically. Hence, the debt is expressed in both domestic (D^{d}) and foreign currencies (D^{f}). The nominal effective exchange rate (e),[35] abbreviated as NEER, is defined as the number of domestic currency units per one unit of foreign currency (direct quotation). Therefore, an increase in e_{t+1} over e_t represents a depreciation of the domestic currency and vice versa. The assumption is depicted in the following equation:

$$D_{t+1} = D_{t+1}^{\mathrm{d}} + e_{t+1} D_{t+1}^{\mathrm{f}} \ .$$

In this case, I assume an open economy and incorporate other flows (stock-flow adjustment and residual term) to achieve a high level of accuracy. Furthermore, the flow budget constraint is defined as follows (for example, refer to IMF, 2013):

$$D_{t+1} = (1 + \varepsilon_{t+1})\left(1 + i_{t+1}^{\mathrm{f}}\right) D_t^{\mathrm{f}} + \left(1 + i_{t+1}^{\mathrm{d}}\right) D_t^{\mathrm{d}} - \mathrm{PB}_{t+1} + \mathrm{SFA}_{t+1} + \mathrm{RES}_{t+1} \ ,$$

where:

- D is the stock of (total) general government debt.
- t is the relevant time period.

(continued)

---

[32] Moreover, such analysis would contain significant uncertainties and future prospects connected with the COVID-19 crisis and the Russian invasion of Ukraine.

[33] For example, see the Fiscal Sustainability Report 2021 (European Commission, 2022b).

[34] For instance, see Piscetek (2019).

[35] I use effective exchange rate due to the heterogeneous debt structure. The assumption of homogeneity—debt denominated only in one foreign currency—is not very plausible. The same argument applies to the interest rates regarding heterogeneous debt structure.

Box 7.2 (continued)

- D^{d} is the stock of local currency-denominated debt.
- D^{f} is the stock of foreign currency-denominated debt.
- ε is the relative change of the NEER, where $1 + \varepsilon_{t+1} = \frac{e_{t+1}}{e_t}$.
- i^{d} is the effective nominal interest rate on D^{d}.
- i^{f} is the effective nominal interest rate on D^{f}.
- PB is the primary balance that is defined as government revenue less non-interest government expenditure.
- SFA (stock-flow adjustment) are other flows that are not included in the government revenues or expenditures but affect the overall debt level.
- RES is the residual term[36] that contains data inconsistencies and/or statistical discrepancy.

Next, I express the previous equation in GDP shares, dividing it by nominal GDP in local currency in period t+1. Moreover, I replace all the relevant variables, except domestic-currency and foreign-currency debt stocks, with small letters denoting the GDP ratios for simplicity. Then, the contributions of the relevant variables can be isolated after several adjustments. Finally, the equation would still contain some nominal variables. Nevertheless, it is more appropriate to use real variables with a more precise economic meaning. Therefore, the final equation can also be expressed in real terms of the effective exchange rate (REER) and the effective interest rate (IMF, 2013):

$$d_{t+1}-d_t=\left(\frac{1}{1+g_{t+1}}\right)$$

$$\times\left[\underbrace{\left(r^{\mathrm{d}}_{t+1}\frac{d^{\mathrm{d}}_t}{d_t}+r^{\mathrm{f}}_{t+1}\frac{d^{\mathrm{f}}_t}{d_t}\right)}_{\substack{\text{Contribution of real}\\ \text{effect. interest rate}}}+\underbrace{d^{\mathrm{f}}_t\xi_{t+1}\left(1+r^{\mathrm{f}}_{t+1}\right)}_{\substack{\text{Contribution}\\ \text{of REER}}}\underbrace{-d_t g_{t+1}}_{\substack{\text{Contr. of real}\\ \text{GDP growth}}}\right]\underbrace{-\mathrm{pb}_{t+1}+\mathrm{sfa}_{t+1}+\mathrm{res}_{t+1}}_{\substack{\text{Contribution of primary balance}\\ \text{and other factors}}},$$

where the partial real effective interest rates (r) are based on the Fisher equation. Moreover, the REER is defined as NEER adjusted for price level difference, ξ represents the changes in REER, and π captures the respective changes in price levels in domestic and foreign economies:

(continued)

[36] I include this term to ensure that the aggregate calculations are identical to the actual data. The issue of inconsistency is explained in the following text. For analytical precision, this term should be as small as possible, which was achieved in the following calculations.

Box 7.2 (continued)

$$\left(1+i_{t+1}^{\mathrm{d}}\right)=\left(1+r_{t+1}^{\mathrm{d}}\right)\left(1+\pi_{t+1}^{\mathrm{d}}\right)$$
$$\left(1+i_{t+1}^{\mathrm{d}}\right)=\left(1+r_{t+1}^{\mathrm{f}}\right)\left(1+\pi_{t+1}^{\mathrm{f}}\right)$$
$$1+\xi_{t+1}=\frac{e_{t+1}}{e_t}\left(\frac{1+\pi_{t+1}^{\mathrm{f}}}{1+\pi_{t+1}^{\mathrm{d}}}\right).$$

Another important dimension is a gap analysis. A debt-stabilising primary balance (pb*) needs to be equal to the automatic debt dynamics.[37] However, it is necessary to be careful. As Escolano (2010) states, the term '*debt-stabilising*' is a misnomer because the stabilisation does not imply reaching the target level of the debt. It solely focuses on keeping the debt-to-GDP ratio constant. Furthermore, the calculation does not consider the stock-flow adjustment and the residual term because these '*exogenous*' flows are irrelevant in this case. Therefore, I assume that the debt-to-GDP ratio does not change ($d_t = d_{t+1}$)

$$\mathrm{pb}_{t+1}^{*}=\left(\frac{1}{1+g_{t+1}}\right)\left[d_t\left(r_{t+1}^{\mathrm{d}}\frac{d_t^{\mathrm{d}}}{d_t}+r_{t+1}^{\mathrm{f}}\frac{d_t^{\mathrm{f}}}{d_t}\right)+d_t^{\mathrm{f}}\xi_{t+1}\left(1+r_{t+1}^{\mathrm{f}}\right)-d_t g_{t+1}\right].$$

7.3.1 Historical Debt Dynamics of the EU4 Countries

The following analysis presents the historical decomposition of general government gross consolidated debt dynamics of the EU4 countries and related indicators analysis. It is based on the actual data of the countries, which include general government consolidated gross debts and their structures, GDP levels, real GDP growths, real interest rates, the real effective exchange rate(s) of the euro against 42 trade-partner countries based on GDP deflator,[38] general government primary budget balances, and stock-flow adjustment measures.

It should be mentioned that there are certain limitations given the more realistic open economy assumptions. The data regarding the general government debt stock structure in foreign-denominated currencies and the respective effective interest rates are unavailable. Hence, the calculations assume that the effective interest rates on domestic- and foreign-denominated debt are identical. Furthermore, the euro is taken

[37] Some authors also consider tax gap, focusing on government revenue. However, I decided not to use this indicator due to the inappropriateness of tax policy in solving debt problems and economic inefficiencies.

[38] The data are obtained from the ECB Warehouse, which uses a different definition of the REER. It is based on an indirect quotation, while the used analytical framework utilises direct quotation. Therefore, I reversed the signs of the original variable to keep it consistent with the concept of direct quotation.

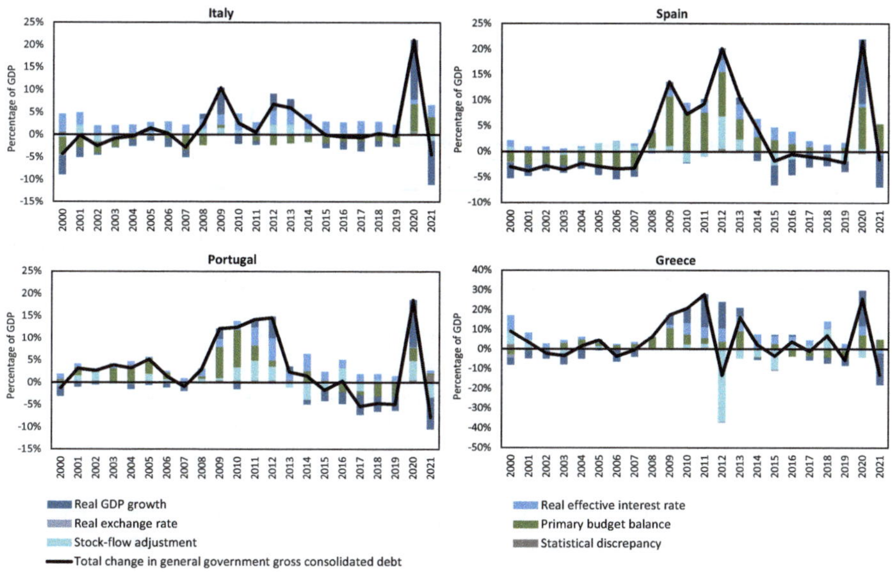

Fig. 7.21 Decomposition of changes in general government gross debt to GDP ratios—EU4, 2000–2021. Source: Own calculations and processing

as the domestic currency.[39] The inaccuracies are rather insignificant and captured in a separate residual term. Furthermore, note that the EU4 countries are participating in a monetary union. Consequently, the distinction between the '*domestic*' and '*foreign*' does not strictly refer to the ownership but the currency denomination aspect.

Figure 7.21 shows a historical decomposition of absolute changes in general government gross debt to GDP of the EU4 countries between 2000 and 2021. First, it is possible to identify the specifics of each of the countries. The automatic debt dynamics (the effects of real effective interest rate, real GDP growth, and REER) were crucial for Italy, Portugal, and Greece. The debt accumulation in Spain was highly determined by primary budget balances, which implies that this country has a larger '*manoeuvring*' space or higher potential for discretionary fiscal measures. The effects of REER were negligible due to the low amounts of foreign currency-denominated debts in the EU4 countries. In addition, a real effective interest rate has been a relatively dominant factor of debt dynamics for Italy during the examined period. Furthermore, the GDP growth effect had been decisive for Greece, while Portugal's contributions to the factors were fairly diversified.

Second, the data also show time-changing patterns. Real effective interest rates had a relatively strong effect before the financial crisis, which implies that the ECB had a strong motivation to reduce the interest rates due to its monetary policy

[39] Greece entered the Euro Area in 2001. Therefore, the calculations for the year 2000 are simplified in this case.

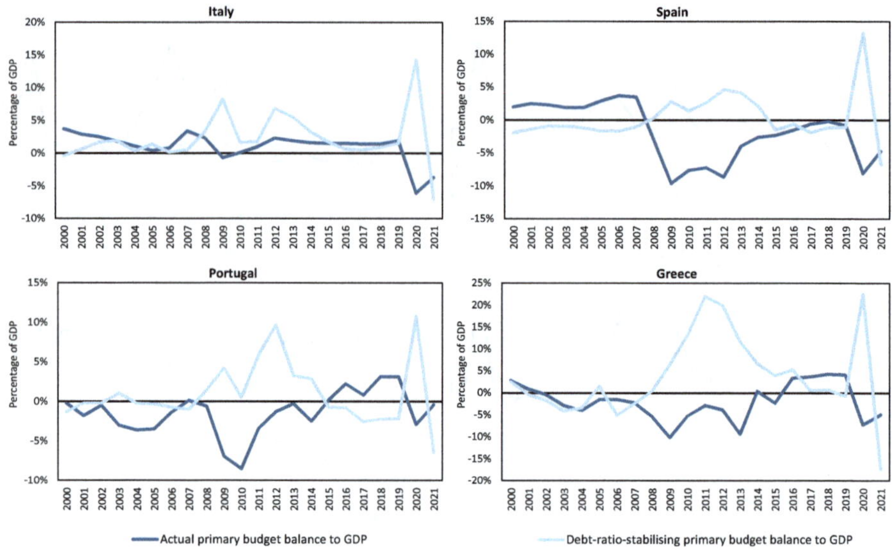

Fig. 7.22 Debt-stabilising general government primary budget balances to GDP and actual primary budget balances to GDP (gap analysis)—EU4, 2000–2021. Source: Eurostat (2022a), own calculations and processing

decisions. Nevertheless, the policy is arguably not sustainable or beneficial in the long term.[40] Moreover, during the initial impact of the financial crisis (between 2008 and 2014), the EU4 countries relied on different strategies. Portugal and Spain decided to counter the negative effects of the crisis by stimulating the economies through primary budget balances. This was not the case for Italy and Greece in terms of relative importance. The former country did not need any financial assistance from the EU, while Greece entered a rescue programme (First Economic Adjustment Programme) in 2012, and a large portion of Greek debt was written off, which is reflected in the stock-flow adjustment.[41]

After 2014, the relative indebtedness of the countries had been reduced by positive GDP growth. However, the effect was much weaker in Greece. Except for Spain, the countries could also reduce their debt levels by reaching primary balance surpluses. Since 2020, the effects of GDP growth and primary balances have been crucial due to the COVID-19 crisis. Note that the GDP growth effects were dominant in all the EU4 countries in 2020.

Figure 7.22 compares debt-stabilising primary balances to the actual primary balances of the EU4 between 2000 and 2021. Note that the debt levels of the EU4 countries were stable (or even declining in Spain), leading to small gaps between the two measures before the financial crisis, while the actual balances were significantly

[40] A detailed discussion is provided in the relevant chapters.

[41] Note that the Greek debt relief was much larger than 36.2% of GDP—the SFA term. However, the stock-flow adjustment captures more factors. It was analysed in the previous text.

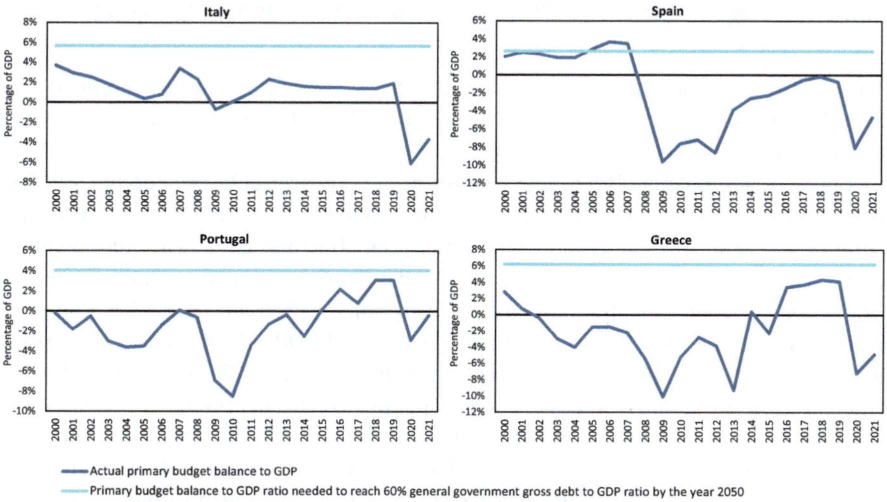

Fig. 7.23 General government primary budget balances to GDP needed to lower debt ratios to 60% by the year 2050 and actual primary budget balances (gap analysis)—EU4, 2000–2021. Note: The estimates of required primary balances are based on debt dynamics equations and assumptions of the development of future values according to their 2000–2021 averages. The assumptions are presented in the following subchapter. Source: Eurostat (2022a), own calculations and processing

different from the debt-stabilising balances between 2008 and 2014 and during the COVID-19 crisis after 2019. Nevertheless, as was mentioned, debt stabilisation is not a sufficient condition in the environment of already high (relative) debt levels, which were recorded in the EU4 countries. The debt-stabilising primary balances represent only an effect needed to counter the debt dynamics or stop the debt ratios from growing.

Moreover, there is no need to eliminate the debts entirely because the costs would be prohibitive. It would probably be sufficient for the countries to comply with the Maastricht criterion of 60%.[42] Therefore, I also show Fig. 7.23, which represents the primary balances needed to bring the relative debt level of each country to 60% of GDP by the year 2050. The calculations are based on the assumption of reaching average values of the relevant variables between 2000 and 2001. It is explained in the next subchapter. The latter figure offers a more precise interpretation of debt sustainability during the examined period. The primary balances of Italy, Portugal, and Greece were insufficient for most of the period, rendering the debt situations unsustainable. The position of Spain was sustainable from this point of view until 2007.

---

[42] The issue was discussed in the second chapter.

7.3.2 Long-Term Debt Projections and Sensitivity Analysis

The next part of the fiscal analysis is a numerical overview and projections of the debt dynamics for each country—based on the analytical framework presented in the previous text.

I present approximately 30-year long-term government debt projections, ranging from 2022 to 2050. The projections assume that the relevant variables for each country would show their average values between 2000 and 2021. This period can be divided into several phases. First, there was an economic expansion characterised by expansionary economic policies and over-optimism. Second, the EU4 countries were significantly affected by the financial crisis of 2008–2009 and needed some time to recover. It led to massive government interventions. Third, 2014–2019 was characterised by a slow recovery accompanied by higher GDP growths, some primary balance surpluses, and debt decreases. Since 2020, the EU4 countries have been significantly hit by the COVID-19 crisis, associated lockdowns, and further instabilities, such as the Russian invasion of Ukraine. In other words, the selected time frame represents the period that started approximately when the Euro Area was created.

Nevertheless, it should be noted that the aim is not to solely replicate the debt dynamics in the given periods. Hence, I also incorporate a sensitivity analysis and explore the effects of various macroeconomic shocks. Note that the analysis ignores the underlying correlations between the variables and possibly endogenous economic policy responses.[43] Furthermore, I assume a linear development for simplicity by using constant values each year in the future. The relaxation of these assumptions would need to include additional and very specific assumptions, making the analysis more complicated, specific scenario-dependent, and less transparent. Finally, note that the analysis aims not to provide accurate forecasts but to show the general long-term trends and analyse the individual drivers of debt dynamics under different circumstances.

Table 7.4 provides an overview of the used variables and their average values for the respective period. It provides several insights. First, nearly all the EU4 debts are stored in the domestic (euro) currency. Second, all the countries, on average, showed primary deficits during the examined period except for Italy. Third, only Spain recorded an average GDP growth of above 1%. Finally, the real effective interest rates for the EU4 countries were around 2%.

The implicit debt dynamics of the countries during the given period are shown in Table 7.5. Positive values represent an increase in the debt-to-GDP ratio. Italy and Greece suffered from significantly negative automatic debt dynamics (snowball effect), leading to debt hoarding even without reaching primary deficits. Italy, on average, showed primary surpluses. However, its debt ratio has been steadily increasing due to the automatic dynamics. In contrast, Spain and Portugal showed

[43] It represents a trade-off between accuracy (stochastic forecast) and rather static analysis (deterministic forecast based on the concept of partial equilibrium).

Table 7.4 Debt dynamics of the EU4 countries—assumed values, 2000–2021 annual averages

Variable	Assumed value	Variable	Assumed value
Italy		*Spain*	
Share of debt in national currency	99.24%	Share of debt in national currency	99.21%
Share of debt in foreign currency	0.86%	Share of debt in foreign currency	0.79%
REER change (+ deprec./– apprec.)	+0.41%	REER change (+ deprec./– apprec.)	+0.41%
Primary balance to GDP	1.05%	Primary balance to GDP	−1.82%
Real GDP growth	0.27%	Real GDP growth	1.41%
Real effective interest rate	2.10%	Real effective interest rate	1.66%
Stock-flow adjustment to GDP	0.37%	Stock-flow adjustment to GDP	0.31%
Statistical discrepancy to GDP	0.15%	Statistical discrepancy to GDP	0.13%
Portugal		*Greece*	
Share of debt in national currency	99.13%	Share of debt in national currency	97.59%
Share of debt in foreign currency	0.87%	Share of debt in foreign currency	2.41%
REER change (+ deprec./– apprec.)	+0.41%	REER change (+ deprec./– apprec.)	+0.41%
Primary balance to GDP	−1.42%	Primary balance to GDP	−2.00%
Real GDP growth	0.70%	Real GDP growth	0.29%
Real effective interest rate	1.57%	Real effective interest rate	2.41%
Stock-flow adjustment to GDP	0.61%	Stock-flow adjustment to GDP	−1.53%
Statistical discrepancy to GDP	0.30%	Statistical discrepancy to GDP	0.29%

Source: Own calculations and processing

relatively better autonomic debt dynamics, but their situations were driven by primary deficits. Note that the effect of the real effective exchange rate was negligible due to very low amounts of government debts denominated in foreign currencies.

Considering all the factors, Fig. 7.24 shows the projected debt ratio developments for the EU4 countries until 2050. The EU4 debt-to-GDP ratios would grow very quickly. The total dynamics are relatively more robust for Greece and Portugal. By 2050, Spain would reach approximately 200% of its GDP, Portugal and Italy would reach approximately 240% of their GDPs, and the Greek general government consolidated gross debt would exceed 380% of its GDP.

Moreover, Fig. 7.25 depicts the sensitivity of the EU4 debt trajectories to macroeconomic shocks. Specifically, it shows reactions of the debt paths to changes in real GDP growth and real effective interest rates under two scenarios for each variable—optimistic and pessimistic variants. I assume constant GDP growth rates of 2.5% to be an optimistic variant as opposed to the growth rate of 0.5%, which is an adverse, however, more realistic outcome. Moreover, I show two borderline variants

Table 7.5 Debt dynamics of the EU4 countries—relative contributions to general government gross debt to GDP ratios

A. Automatic debt dynamics

Country	Real effective interest rate effect (1)	Real GDP growth effect (2)	Real effective exchange rate (REER) effect (3)	Total effect (1+2+3)
Italy	2.09%	−0.27%	0.00%	1.82%
Spain	1.64%	−1.39%	0.00%	0.24%
Portugal	1.56%	−0.69%	0.00%	0.87%
Greece	2.40%	−0.29%	+0.01%	2.11%

B. Other factors of debt dynamics

Country	Average primary balance (4)	Average stock-flow adjustment (5)	Average statistical discrepancy (6)	Total debt dynamics (1+2+3+4+5+6)
Italy	−0.56 ppts	0.20 ppts	0.08 ppts	1.82% − 0.28 ppts
Spain	1.18 ppts	0.20 ppts	0.08 ppts	0.24% + 1.46 ppts
Portugal	0.80 ppts	0.35 ppts	0.17 ppts	0.87% + 1.31 ppts
Greece	0.74 ppts	−0.56 ppts	0.11 ppts	2.11% + 0.28 ppts

Note: Some numbers do not add up due to rounding off
Source: Own calculations and processing

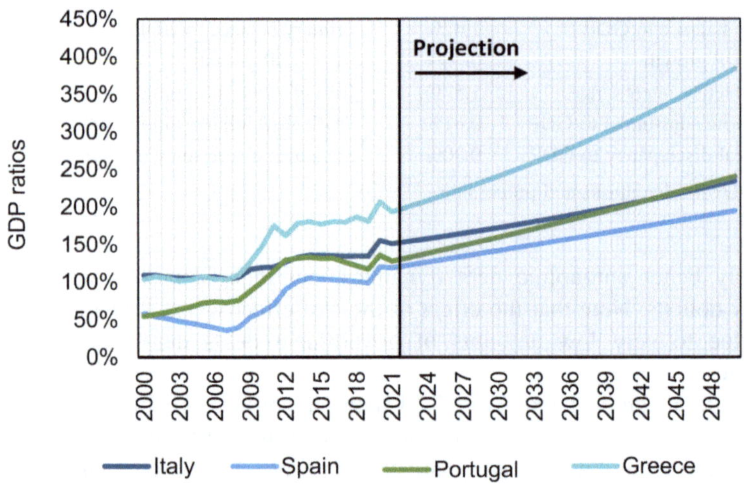

Fig. 7.24 Development of general government gross debt to GDP ratios—EU4, 2000–2050. Source: Own calculations and processing

of real effective interest rates. Considering the past policies of negative interest rates, I show the effects of slightly negative real effective interest rates of −0.5%, which is a favourable scenario regarding the government debt level.

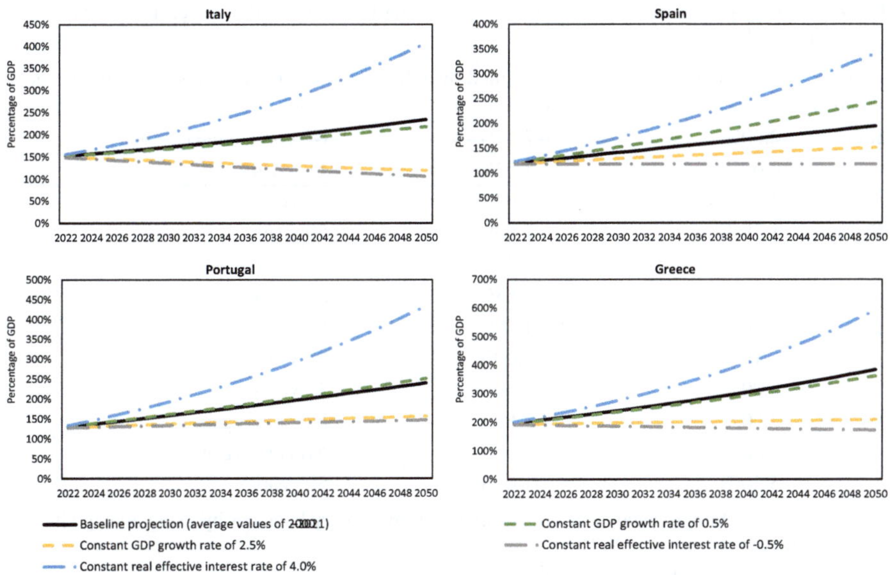

Fig. 7.25 Sensitivity analysis—impact of real GDP growth rates and real effective interest rates on debt ratios—EU4, 2022–2050. Source: Own calculations and processing

At the same time, I present relatively high values of real effective interest rates reaching 4%. I decided to use a higher value due to a possible rise of a risk premium in the future.[44]

Note that the exchange rate effects are not depicted because they are negligible due to low values of foreign-currency (non-euro) denominated debts. The data show that high interest rates would be detrimental to all the EU4 countries. The fact shapes the monetary policy of the ECB.[45] Surprisingly, even very optimistic values of GDP growth at 2.5% and real effective interest rates at −0.5% would not be able to bring the debt-to-GDP ratios down noticeably, except for Italy. In addition, the most problematic situation is in Greece, which shows extremely high values, followed by the situation in Spain because GDP growth has a relatively low impact on its debt-to-GDP ratio.

Arguably, the debt situations of the EU countries would not be sustainable if the countries exhibited 2000–2021 average values of the relevant indicators in the next 30 years approximately. It cannot be expected that the countries would be able to improve their positions under the given circumstances significantly. Nevertheless, Spain and Portugal have a relatively larger manoeuvring space for improving their situation by adjusting their budget balances.

[44] For example, Greece had already shown substantially higher (double-digit) interest rates during and after the financial crisis of 2008–2009.

[45] For a more detailed discussion, refer to the issue of fiscal dominance presented in the third chapter.

Table 7.6 Projected general government gross budget balances needed to reach 60% of debt to GDP ratios—EU4 countries

Country	Assumed primary balance	Assumed overall balance	Number of years to reach 60% debt ratio
Italy	2.00%	−2.52%	No convergence
	3.00%	−1.52%	113 years
	3.88%	−0.64%	50 years
Spain	1.39%	−1.03%	50 years
	2.00%	−0.42%	33 years
	3.00%	0.58%	22 years
Portugal	2.00%	−1.39%	59 years
	2.19%	−1.20%	50 years
	3.00%	−0.39%	32 years
Greece	2.00%	−2.59%	No convergence
	3.00%	−1.59%	No convergence
	5.60%	1.01%	50 years

Note: The overall budget balances were calculated from primary balances by using average interest payments between 2000 and 2021
Source: Own calculations and processing

Finally, we might be interested in the budget balances, which could bring the EU4 debt-to-GDP ratios to appropriate levels. Therefore, Table 7.6 shows the number of years needed to reach 60% of general government debt to GDP ratio (Maastricht criterion level) for different levels of primary balances.

Italy and Greece are in relatively more difficult situations. Greece will arguably be unable to keep a balanced budget for the next 50 years, therefore not reaching the ratio. It would be significantly at odds with its historical behaviour. The situation in Italy is similar, although slightly better. Finally, Spain and Portugal are in relatively better positions regarding the required sizes of budget balances. The latter country would be able to run overall deficits of 1.20% of its GDP and still be able to lower the debt-to-GDP ratio to 60% in 50 years.

References

Bank of Italy. (2022). *Statistical data*. Retrieved June 26, 2022, from https://www.bancaditalia.it/

Bank of Portugal. (2022). *Statistical data*. Retrieved June 26, 2022, from https://www.bportugal.pt/

Baxter, M., & King, R. G. (1999). Measuring business cycles: Approximate band-pass filters for economic time series. *Review of Economics and Statistics, 81*(4), 575–593.

Beveridge, S., & Nelson, C. R. (1981). A new approach to decomposition of economic time series into permanent and transitory components with particular attention to measurement of the business cycle. *Journal of Monetary Economics, 7*(2), 151–174.

Blejer, M. I., & Cheasty, A. (1993). *How to measure the fiscal deficit: Analytical and methodological issues*. International Monetary Fund. https://doi.org/10.5089/9781557751928.071. ISBN: 978-1557751928.

Bornhorst, F., et al. (2011). *When and how to adjust beyond the business cycle? A guide to structural fiscal balances* (Technical Notes and Manuals). International Monetary Fund. Retrieved April 25, 2022, from https://www.imf.org/en/Publications/TNM/Issues/2016/12/31/When-and-How-to-Adjust-Beyond-the-Business-Cycle-A-Guide-to-Structural-Fiscal-Balances-24787

Buti, M., et al. (2019). *Potential output and EU fiscal surveillance*. VOX EU – CEPR. Retrieved April 20, 2022, from https://voxeu.org/article/potential-output-and-eu-fiscal-surveillance

Chalaux, T., & Guillemette, Y. (2019). *The OECD potential output estimation methodology* (IMF Working Paper No. 1563). International Monetary Fund. Retrieved April 16, 2022, from https://bit.ly/3gy8Zok

Christiano, L. J., & Fitzgerald, T. J. (2003). The band pass filter. *International Economic Review, 44*(2), 435–465.

Debrun, X., et al. (2018). *Debt sustainability* (IMF Conference Paper). International Monetary Fund. Retrieved June 11, 2022, from https://www.imf.org/-/media/Files/News/Seminars/2018/091318SovDebt-conference/chapter-4-debt-sustainability.ashx

EU Independent Fiscal Institutions Network (EUIFIN). (2018). *A practitioner's guide to potential output and the output gap* (Tech. Rep.). Retrieved April 25, 2022, from https://www.euifis.eu/download/ogwg_paper.pdf

European Central Bank (ECB). (2022). *ECB statistical data warehouse*. Retrieved September 4, 2022, from https://sdw.ecb.europa.eu/

European Commission. (2022a). *AMECO database*. Retrieved August 14, 2022, from https://ec.europa.eu/economy_finance/ameco

European Commission. (2022b). *Fiscal sustainability report 2021*. Retrieved August 05, 2022, from https://economy-finance.ec.europa.eu/publications/fiscal-sustainability-report-2021_en

Eurostat. (2022a). *Eurostat database*. Retrieved September 21, 2022, from https://ec.europa.eu/eurostat

Eurostat. (2022b). *Macroeconomic imbalance procedure scoreboard*. Retrieved July 1, 2022, from https://ec.europa.eu/eurostat/web/macroeconomic-imbalances-procedure/data/scoreboard

Escolano, J. (2010). *A practical guide to public debt dynamics, fiscal sustainability, and cyclical adjustment of budgetary aggregates* (Technical Note and Manual No. 2010/02). International Monetary Fund. Retrieved May 28, 2022, from https://www.imf.org/external/pubs/ft/tnm/2010/tnm1002.pdf

Grant, A. L., & Chan, J. C. (2017a). Reconciling output gaps: Unobserved components model and Hodrick–Prescott filter. *Journal of Economic Dynamics and Control, 75*, 114–121. https://doi.org/10.1016/j.jedc.2016.12.004

Grant, A. L., & Chan, J. C. C. (2017b). A Bayesian model comparison for trend-cycle decompositions of output. *Journal of Money, Credit and Banking, 49*(2–3), 525–552.

Grant, A. L., & Chan, J. C. C. (2017c). *Measuring the output gap using stochastic model specification search* (Working Paper). Retrieved March 15, 2022, from https://joshuachan.org/papers/output-gap-SMSS.pdf

Gualtieri, R. (2019). *Response to the concerns regarding the 2020 Draft Budgetary Plan (DBP)*. Retrieved April 28, 2022, from https://ec.europa.eu/info/sites/info/files/economy-finance/minister_gualtieri_-_letter_to_ec_23_10_2019_1.pdf

Hamilton, J. D. (2018). Why you should never use the Hodrick-Prescott filter. *Review of Economics and Statistics, 100*(5), 831–843.

Hodrick, R. J., & Prescott, E. C. (1997). Postwar U.S. business cycles: An empirical investigation. *Journal of Money, Credit and Banking, 29*(1), 1–16.

Hristov, A., Raciborski, R., & Vandermeulen, V. (2017). *Assessment of the plausibility of the output gap estimates* (Economic Brief No. 023). Retrieved April 24, 2022, from https://ec.europa.eu/info/sites/info/files/eb023_en.pdf

International Monetary Fund (IMF). (2005). *Italy: 2004 Article IV consultation* (IMF Country Report No. 05/44). Retrieved April 20, 2022, from https://www.imf.org/external/pubs/ft/scr/2005/cr0544.pdf

International Monetary Fund (IMF). (2013). *Staff guidance note for public debt sustainability analysis in market-access countries* (Tech. Rep.). International Monetary Fund. Retrieved May 28, 2022, from https://www.imf.org/external/np/pp/eng/2013/050913.pdf

International Monetary Fund (IMF). (2016). *Portugal: Ex-post evaluation of exceptional access under the 2011 extended arrangement* (IMF Country Report No. 16/302). Retrieved April 20, 2022, from https://www.imf.org/external/pubs/ft/scr/2016/cr16302.pdf

International Monetary Fund (IMF). (2017). *Greece: 2016 Article IV consultation* (IMF Country Report No. 17/40). Retrieved April 20, 2022, from https://www.imf.org/~/media/Files/Publications/CR/2017/cr1740.ashx

International Monetary Fund (IMF). (2022). *World economic outlook database*. Retrieved August 15, 2022, from https://www.imf.org/en/Publications/WEO

Kamber, G., Morley, J., & Wong, B. (2018). Intuitive and reliable estimates of the output gap from a Beveridge-Nelson filter. *The Review of Economics and Statistics, 100*(3), 550–566.

Kremer, J., et al. (2006). *A disaggregated framework for the analysis of structural developments in public finances* (ECB Working Paper No. 579). European Central Bank. Retrieved April 25, 2022, from https://www.ecb.europa.eu/pub/pdf/scpwps/ecbwp579.pdf

Koen, V., & Noord, P. v. d. (2005). *Fiscal gimmickry in Europe: One-off measures and creative accounting* (OECD Economics Department Working Paper No. 417). Organisation for Economic Co-Operation and Development (OECD). Retrieved April 22, 2022, from https://www.oecd-ilibrary.org/docserver/237714513517.pdf

Kožić, I., & Sever, I. (2014). Measuring business cycles: Empirical mode decomposition of economic time series. *Economics Letters, 123*(3), 287–290.

Mourre, G., Astarita, C., & Princen, S. (2014). *Adjusting the budget balance for the business cycle: The EU methodology* (Economic Paper No. 536). Retrieved April 24, 2022, from https://ec.europa.eu/economy_finance/publications/economic_paper/2014/pdf/ecp536_en.pdf

Mourre, G., Poissonnier, A., & Lausegger, M. (2019). *The semi-elasticities underlying the cyclically-adjusted budget balance: An update & further analysis* (Discussion Paper No. 098). Retrieved April 24, 2022, from https://ec.europa.eu/info/sites/info/files/economy-finance/dp098_ en.pdf

Organisation for Economic Co-operation and Development (OECD). (2012). *OECD economic surveys: Spain 2012* (Tech. Rep.). Retrieved April 20, 2022, from https://www.oecd-ilibrary.org/economics/oecd-economic-surveys-spain-2012_eco_surveys-esp-2012-en

Organisation for Economic Co-operation and Development (OECD). (2017). Financial net worth of general government. In *Government at a glance 2017*. OECD Publishing. https://doi.org/10.1787/gov_glance-2017-12-en

Organisation for Economic Co-operation and Development (OECD). (2022). *Economic Outlook Database*. Retrieved August 20, 2022, from https://stats.oecd.org/

PDMA Greece – Greek Public Debt Management Agency. (2022). *Statistical data*. Retrieved June 26, 2022, from http://www.pdma.gr/

Percival, D. B., & Walden, A. T. (2008). *Wavelet methods for time series analysis*. Cambridge University Press.

Piscetek, M. (2019). *Public debt dynamics in New Zealand* (Working Paper No. 19/01). New Zealand Treasury. Retrieved May 28, 2022, from https://treasury.govt.nz/sites/default/files/2019-07/twp19-01.pdf

Spanish Ministry of Finance. (2022). *Statistical data*. Retrieved June 26, 2022, from https://www.tesoro.es/en

Xafa, M. (2014). *Lessons from the 2012 Greek debt restructuring* (VoxEU Article). The Centre for Economic Policy Research (CEPR). Retrieved June 30, 2022, from https://voxeu.org/article/greek-debt-restructuring-lessons-learned

Chapter 8
Long-Term Determinants and Efficiency of Fiscal Policies

The next parts of the text aim to identify and describe the determinants and efficiency of the fiscal policies of the EU4 countries. These findings should improve the understanding of the countries' fiscal policymaking. Nevertheless, it should be mentioned that there is a fair degree of uncertainty concerning the estimates. The results should be interpreted with caution. Hence, the following text focuses on general patterns rather than on (im)precise quantitative interpretations. Finally, the presented estimates were made using the same methodology for all the countries. This fact makes the estimates comparable,[1] but the trade-off implies that they are less focused on fitting country-specific time series.

This chapter has two parts. The first part deals with fiscal determinants. It presents estimates of fiscal reaction functions using error correction (EC) models. The second part focuses on estimating fiscal multipliers, which are used for the efficiency evaluation of the EU4 fiscal policies. In this regard, advanced Bayesian vector autoregressive (BVAR) models are employed.

8.1 Fiscal Reaction Functions

A fiscal reaction function is a workhorse model approach used to capture fiscal behaviour and its determinants. It describes the systematic response of primary budget balance to relevant variables in annual terms.[2] Hence, it is a positive approach focusing on the empirical description of average patterns in fiscal policy choices (Burger et al., 2011). The primary budget balance is predominantly used as the explained variable due to its direct observability and exclusion of interest

[1]The comparability is a feature that is very difficult to find in expert literature.

[2]The annual data are the most fitting due to the time lags and legislative processes because government budgets are usually planned for 1 year in advance.

M. Bednář, *Fiscal Policy in the Southern European Union Countries*, Contributions to Finance and Accounting, https://doi.org/10.1007/978-3-031-29761-8_8

payments, which would bias the interpretation of the estimates. Furthermore, a wide range of explanatory variables may be used. For instance, the level of government debt, the state of the business cycle, or other economic and even political variables. Nevertheless, the fiscal responses are subject to the socio-economic environment—both global and country-specific. Therefore, fiscal responses are bound to be considerably volatile and country-specific, making the identification of fiscal determinants difficult.

The empirical literature concerning estimating the EU fiscal reaction functions primarily focuses on panel data and fiscal sustainability.[3] Nevertheless, this analysis aims to capture country-specific reactions. Hence, the panel data approach, which averages the individual effects, is unsuitable. To my knowledge, no comprehensive study has been made that would individually focus on the EU4 fiscal reactions. Legrenzi and Milas (2013) estimated state-varying thresholds of fiscal policy reaction functions for the GIPS countries; however, they examined Ireland instead of Italy.

Moreover, the authors focused on fiscal sustainability rather than fiscal policy determinants. The most relevant study was probably made by Berti et al. (2016), who estimated individual fiscal reaction functions of selected EU countries for the European Commission. Therefore, the following estimation procedure employs their methodology.

Box 8.1 Error Correction Models: Used Methodology

The derivation of a fiscal reaction function is based on the debt dynamics equations used in the previous chapter. To be specific, it exploits the long-term relationship between primary balance to GDP and debt to GDP ratios:

$$\frac{\mathrm{PB}_t}{Y_t} = \alpha + \beta \frac{\mathrm{Debt}_{t-1}}{Y_{t-1}} + \varepsilon_t,$$

where PB is the primary balance, debt is the overall general government consolidated gross debt, Y is total output or GDP, and ε is the error term. In other words, the level of primary balance is explained by the overall debt level in the previous period. If the debt-to-GDP ratio increases, the government should respond by improving the primary balance to counter the increase in the debt ratio. It represents an error-correction mechanism (see Bohn, 1998).

It should be noted that an inverse long-term relationship also exists—the reaction of debt level to primary balance. However, I use a simple one-way error-correction mechanism to make the separate country estimations as transparent and comparable as possible. The approach contrasts with more

(continued)

[3] This is done through the inclusion of a debt coefficient that captures the response of primary balance to the overall debt level.

Box 8.1 (continued)
complicated vector error correction models (VECM) where structural identification would need to be made. Nevertheless, the models utilise lagged debt ratio and relevant lagged explanatory variables to capture fiscal behaviour and avoid endogeneity. The adjustments are in line with the methodology of Berti et al. (2016) regarding the European Commission's estimates.

In the next step, the fiscal reaction equation is adjusted according to the error-correction procedure. Nevertheless, it is estimated in one step using the methodology of Banerjee et al. (1998). The fiscal reaction function is specified as follows:

$$\Delta \text{pb}_t = \alpha + \rho(\text{pb}_{t-1} - \text{adebt}_{t-2}) + \beta \Delta \text{debt}_{t-1} + \varepsilon_t,$$

where small letters denote the relevant GDP ratios, and ρ is the error-correction term that should be a statistically significant value between zero and a negative one. Moreover, the error-correction mechanism represents a long-term relationship, while the other variables outside the parentheses capture short-term fiscal reactions.

The previous equation serves only as a baseline. The model specification for each country is augmented by including more variables. The additional fiscal variables (controls) include the output gap, change in real interest payments on debt, and the primary expenditure gap. Moreover, dummy (binary) variables denote important events—capturing structural breaks in the data. The dummy variables common for each country include World War I, the Great Depression, World War II, Euro Area Accession, the financial crisis of 2008–2009, and the coronavirus crisis of 2020–2021.

Moreover, a model for each country has one unique characteristic: the inclusion of one dummy variable capturing a country-specific event.[4] One of the specific aims is to capture different responses of the EU4 countries since the Euro Area accessions and during the financial crisis of 2008–2009. Hence, the lagged debt to GDP variables is multiplied by the relevant dummy variables.[5]

The models employ annual data and include dummy variables capturing changes at the end of the sample. Hence, the estimation procedure needs a sufficient number of observations, especially before the primary examined period, to obtain representative effects. The main source of data is the Public

(continued)

[4]Italy: Years of Lead (1969–1986), Spain: Transition to democracy (1980–1989), Portugal: 1970s and Carnation Revolution (1970–1979), and Greece: Greco-Turkish War (1897–1898).

[5]With the exception of the COVID-19 crisis due to low number of observations at the end of the sample.

Box 8.1 (continued)
Finances in Modern History Dataset provided by the IMF (2022). Moreover, it also utilises data from Eurostat (2022) and St. Louis Fed (2022). In addition, all the values starting from 2000 were updated using the estimates presented in the previous chapters.

Furthermore, some observations in the middle of the sample were missing. I decided to impute the data by using a Kalman smoother within a state-space representation of automatically selected ARIMA models according to Akaike information criteria. CPI country-specific data are not available until 1960. Hence, the estimation procedure employs the CPI of the USA, provided by Shiller (2022), as a proxy.

Primary government expenditure haps were estimated using the HP filter with the lambda parameter of 100. Moreover, the output gaps were estimated using a univariate unobserved components model. The model decomposes the time series into a cyclical and trend component following Grant and Chan (2017). The cyclical component is modelled as a zero-mean stationary AR (2) process, while the non-stationary trend component is considered to follow a second-order Markov process.[6] The univariate model is used because of a lack of additional data. However, as was mentioned, the dataset starting from 2000 was updated. The values of output gaps are estimated using the trivariate UC model, which was employed in the previous chapter.

The variables in the EC models need to fulfil some assumptions. Most prominently, the primary balances and debt ratios should be integrated in the same order. Furthermore, the other variables need to be stationary to obtain unbiased estimates. According to the relevant statistical test, all the short-term effect variables are stationary, while the primary balances and debt ratios are rather non-stationary. The latter is in line with the theoretical requirements. However, it should be mentioned that the tests showed mixed evidence in some cases. It was also the case of the research made by Berti et al. (2016) for the European Commission. The existence of the long-term relationships between primary balances and relative debt levels was tested by the Engle–Granger cointegration tests. I have verified the validity, as all the tests indicate cointegration between the two variables in the given causal direction. Finally, the regression output utilises Newey-West HAC standard errors to allow for heteroskedasticity and autocorrelation of model residuals.

The results are presented in Table 8.1. The estimates of constants in the models, which are difficult to interpret, might indicate that Greece was more prone to produce deficits when compared to the other EU4 countries. The EC terms are statistically significant and negative between zero and one. Hence, the error-correction

[6] Refer to Grant and Chan (2017) for additional details. The authors entitled the model as the '*UCUR-2M*'.

Table 8.1 Estimates of error correction models—EU4, 1884–2021

	Dependent variable: Δpb			
Independent variables	Italy	Spain	Portugal	Greece
Constant	0.092 (0.407)	−0.100 (0.182)	0.133 (0.343)	−1.535[a] (0.729)
Primary balance (−1) – EC term	−0.164[a] (0.096)	−0.235[c] (0.072)	−0.186[b] (0.063)	−0.147[b] (0.052)
Debt to GDP (−2)	0.008 (0.005)	0.010[c] (0.003)	0.003 (0.008)	0.025[c] (0.007)
Debt to GDP (−2) * Euro Area	0.020 (0.017)	0.004 (0.009)	0.026[b] (0.010)	0.044[c] (0.009)
Debt to GDP (−2) * FC	0.023 (0.023)	0.063[c] (0.016)	0.001 (0.021)	−0.052[c] (0.019)
Debt to GDP change (−1)	−0.009 (0.012)	0.027[a] (0.015)	0.006 (0.065)	0.048[a] (0.025)
Output gap (−1)	−0.050 (0.053)	0.005 (0.012)	0.035 (0.030)	0.051[b] (0.022)
Real interest rate change (−1)	−0.101 (0.067)	0.014 (0.011)	0.039[b] (0.016)	−0.018 (0.031)
Primary expenditure gap (-1)	0.766[c] (0.275)	0.388[c] (0.083)	0.497[c] (0.125)	0.842[c] (0.109)
Euro Area dummy	−2.929 (1.960)	−0.347 (0.840)	−2.089[c] (0.563)	−6.864[c] (1.157)
Financial crisis (FC) dummy	−3.475 (2.588)	−5.622[c] (0.832)	−1.949 (2.217)	−4.196[a] (2.335)
Coronavirus crisis dummy	−3.888[c] (0.970)	−3.626[c] (1.028)	−2.785[c] (0.941)	−8.011[c] (0.907)
World War I dummy	−10.826[c] (0.648)	−0.920[c] (0.145)	−1.254[c] (0.300)	0.532 (0.402)
Great Depression dummy	−0.210 (0.628)	−0.247 (0.213)	−0.129 (0.240)	−1.514 (1.446)
World War II dummy	−9.193[c] (0.460)	−1.948[c] (0.425)	−0.146 (0.158)	−0.777 (0.574)
Country-specific event dummy	−2.502[c] (0.503)	−0.659[b] (0.331)	−1.114[a] (0.633)	−19.331[c] (0.950)
Number of observations:	138	138	138	138
Adjusted R^2:	0.608	0.385	0.274	0.618
ADF test (basic specif., 1 lag):	−15.27[c]	−13.37[c]	−12.83[c]	−12.56[c]
Breusch-Godfrey LM test (1 lag):	19.411[c]	5.549[b]	3.698[a]	1.509

Notes: Newey-West HAC standard errors are in parentheses
Source: Own calculations and processing
[a]$p < 0.1$; [b]$p < 0.05$; [c]$p < 0.01$

mechanisms are estimated adequately. Spain showed the fastest rate of convergence in the gross debt and primary balance relationship, while Greece showed the slowest pace. It indicates that debt increases in Greece and the relevant economic instabilities had relatively high inertia, which is not favourable.

Further, the long-term relationship between lagged debt to GDP and the primary balance to GDP ratio is significant for Spain and Greece. Greece and Spain exhibit noticeable government responses to rising government debt in the long run, unlike the other two countries. The effect was strengthened by the financial crisis of 2008–2009. However, Greece showed negative signs, attributing higher debt to higher budget deficits and lower surpluses. It might represent the specific weak position of Greece during the financial crisis. Further, there is evidence that The Euro Area accession partly stimulated the long-term behaviour of the smaller economies of Portugal and Greece in terms of improved reactions to higher debt by increasing their primary balances. However, the effect is rather weak when compared to the overall effect of the Euro Area dummy variable accession.

The short-term effects of debt ratio changes are only significant for Spain and Greece. The conclusions are similar to the long-term case explained above. Furthermore, the reaction of primary balance changes to the output gap (business cycle) is significant only for Greece. The country showed a positive value, which (on average) indicates that Greece showed some anti-cyclical efforts during the examined period.[7] At the same time, the other countries did not adopt a systematic budget policy in relation to a business cycle. Nevertheless, primary balances do not necessarily reflect government efforts. Moreover, the GDP data are often revised, and the historical values may be less precise.

The reaction to change in real interest payments is significant in the case of Portugal. The value is positive, linking higher interest payments to a lower deficit or higher surplus efforts, which could indicate anticyclical efforts. Arguably, interest payments were a key factor influencing budget balances in Portugal. Furthermore, the primary expenditure gap captures the cyclical nature of government expenditure, or the relevant inertia. The relevant coefficients of all the countries showed high economic and statistical significance. The positive coefficients of the primary expenditure gap indicate that higher government expenditure led to lower budget deficits or higher budget surpluses in the subsequent period. This effect was particularly strong in Greece and Italy. In all the EU4 countries, government expenditures and their deviations from the trend were key determinants of future budget balances.

The overall dummy variable for the Euro Area accession shows highly (statistically and economically) significant negative values for the smaller countries of Portugal and Greece. Arguably, the Euro Area accession motivated the smaller countries to become 'black passengers' by running higher fiscal deficits. The estimates show that the effect of the Euro Area accession was strongly detrimental to Greece. At the same time, the two other larger countries do not show statistically significant results. The estimates might indicate that the supranational fiscal regulations in the Euro Area were useless in this regard. Arguably, the smaller countries (Portugal and Greece) exploited the socialisation of risk in the Euro Area far more than the other two larger countries. The last dummy variable relevant for the analysis

[7] However, note that the partial effect was offset by other factors.

is the variable capturing the COVID-19 crisis and related lockdowns between 2020 and 2021.

It should be noted that Greece showed the most vigorous response to the adverse shock of the COVID-19 crisis, the same as in the case of the previous financial crisis. It is possibly associated with Greece exhibiting higher financial and economic vulnerabilities compared to the other EU4 countries. Nevertheless, the COVID-19 crisis significantly hit all the EU4 countries. However, Spain showed a greater fiscal policy reaction to the previous financial crisis, consistent with the descriptive statistics.[8]

8.2 Fiscal Multipliers

A crucial aspect of fiscal policy is its efficiency. If a fiscal policy has low efficiency, then even the best-planned policy is useless because it cannot significantly affect the critical macroeconomic variables. As a result, it further increases economic instabilities by wasting resources.

The efficiency is traditionally examined by fiscal multipliers, which capture the effects of various fiscal items on main macroeconomic variables. Various fiscal multipliers can be defined depending on the used budgetary items, level of aggregation, lags in fiscal policy effectiveness, and other factors. In this case, the analysis focuses on one of the most widely used multipliers, which shows the effect of government expenditure on total output or GDP. The multiplier shows the change in total output if government expenditure increases by one.

On the one hand, the Keynesian approach to government expenditure multipliers assumes that a certain proportion of economic resources is unemployed and, thus, that a certain fraction of the population is liquidity constrained or economically myopic (Afonso & Leal, 2019). As a result, fiscal stimulus results in higher employment, creating a higher demand. In this perspective, the relevant multiplier is higher than one. On the other hand, the Neoclassical perspective assumes that the economy is in equilibrium and the economic resources are allocated optimally. Hence, an increase in government expenditure crowds out private expenditure, and the relevant fiscal multiplier is between zero and one (Hall, 2009).[9] The standard interpretation is that public expenditure is relatively inefficient compared to private expenditure if the relevant multiplier is lower than one.

Nevertheless, fiscal multipliers are likely to change over time. Fiscal policy is usually more efficient during recessions than expansions (Afonso & Leal, 2019). The size of fiscal multipliers depends on the current stage of a business cycle,

[8] According to the Eurostat (2022), Spain showed a government budget deficit of 11.3% of GDP in 2009 while a deficit of only 10.3% of GDP in 2020.

[9] A shock in government expenditure can increase private investment only if the shock is sufficiently persistent and taxes are sufficiently non-distortionary (Afonso & Leal, 2019).

structural changes in the economy, and external conditions concerning economic openness. According to Batini et al. (2014), DSGE simulations and SVAR models suggest that first-year multipliers generally lie between zero and one in '*normal times*'.[10] Nevertheless, the results have been challenged by more recent literature. In '*abnormal circumstances*', the multipliers can exceed the value of one. In particular, it may occur when the economy is in a severe recession or if the use and/or the transmission of monetary policy are impaired (ibid.).

Several studies confirm the theoretical insight that a fiscal stimulus is less efficient during expansion and more efficient in recession. Thus, the studies show higher values of multipliers in the latter case (see Batini et al., 2014; Warmedinger et al., 2015; Afonso & Leal, 2019). Furthermore, high-debt countries have lower multipliers because the fiscal stimulus is likely to induce adverse credibility and confidence effects on private demand and risk premium (see Senekovič et al., 2019; Afonso & Leal, 2019). The research of Ilzetzki et al. (2011) shows even negative multipliers for highly indebted countries. The authors claim that the multipliers are relatively higher in industrial countries and economies operating under predetermined exchange rates. At the same time, fiscal multipliers are relatively lower in open economies than in closed economies. Kempa and Khan (2015) state that expenditure multipliers are lower in the Euro Area when compared to the other EU countries. In addition, the authors conclude that the multipliers are lower due to the introduction of the euro currency and are higher in the Euro Area periphery than in the EU core countries. Another strand of empirical research argues that the government spending multiplier is significantly higher when interest rates are at, or near, a zero lower bound (Miyamoto et al., 2018).[11] However, the results are inconclusive. Amendola et al. (2019) show that the results do not hold for the Euro Area.

The models aim to estimate the effects of government expenditure on total output in the EU4 countries. I need to impose relatively sophisticated methods to obtain the values of the fiscal multipliers. Moreover, I use a coherent (identical) framework for all the examined countries to achieve comparability of the results.[12] It should be noted that the presented estimates are based on strong assumptions fit for the specific purpose. Therefore, the results should be interpreted with caution.[13]

[10]The estimates are driven by used methodology and data. For instance, these factors include the type of used model, model estimation, data pre-processing, time range, and related issues.

[11]Some authors mention the so-called *Effective Lower Bound* (ELB) due to the introduction of negative interest rates. The ELB is defined as the point beyond which further monetary policy in the same direction is counterproductive (Amendola et al., 2019).

[12]It should be mentioned that there is a trade-off between the comparability and accuracy of the estimates.

[13]The estimations can be performed by using various combinations of different approaches. There is no consensus on which approach is the most suitable one.

Box 8.2 Bayesian Vector Autoregressive Models: Used Methodology
The analysis employs a widely used structural vector autoregressive model framework estimated by Bayesian methods (BVAR models).[14] VAR models are based on the works of the Nobel Memorial Prize in Economic Sciences laureate Christopher A. Sims who proposed the framework as an alternative to the standard econometric models used at that time. The framework is popular in empirical macroeconomics because of its relative simplicity and superior performance. In short, it represents a system of equations (variables) explained by their lagged values and other endogenous variables. VAR model results are routinely used as a benchmark for structural DSGE models used by many central banks worldwide. A detailed description of VAR models, including their estimation and identification methods, is provided by Kilian and Lütkepohl (2017).

The presented BVAR model specifications are based on the seminal work of Blanchard and Perotti (2002), modified by Caldara and Kamps (2008). The used models utilise five macroeconomic variables: government expenditure gap (g_t), output gap (x_t), inflation rate measured by CPI (year-over-year changes; π_t), government revenue gap (r_t), and nominal short-term (3-month) market interest rate (i_t). The estimations utilise quarterly data of the EU4 countries between 2000 and 2021. The values of the gaps were deflated by using HICP with the base year of 2021. These gaps represent an absolute deviation of the relevant variables from their steady-state values. Moreover, a seasonal adjustment of the variables was performed by using the standardised X-13-ARIMA procedure.

The estimations were performed in levels to obtain the values of expenditure multipliers. For this purpose, the estimations work with cyclical components of the relevant variables. The output gap data drawn from the previous estimates are based on the trivariate UC model methodology developed by Grant and Chan (2017).[15] The gaps in government revenue and expenditure were estimated using a seminal univariate UC model decomposition based on Harvey (1985) and Clark (1987). In this regard, the time series are decomposed into trend and cyclical components. Furthermore, the specifications assume that the variables have a direct effect lasting two quarters.

(continued)

[14] The Bayesian econometric techniques significantly differ from the standard frequentist approach. In the Bayesian framework, every parameter of interest is treated as a random variable characterised by some underlying probability distribution. The distribution needs to be estimated to carry the inference on the models. The traditional (frequentist) approach assumes that the estimated parameters have a '*true*' value that needs to be identified. In other words, the Bayesian approach treats parameters as random variables and the observed data as fixed variables.

[15] Refer to the previous chapters.

Box 8.2 (continued)
Therefore, they include two lags of used variables. For each country and period, the following model is estimated:

$$y_t = b_0 + B_1 y_{t-1} + B_2 y_{t-2} + A\varepsilon_t,$$

where:

$$y_t = \begin{pmatrix} g_t \\ x_t \\ \pi_t \\ r_t \\ i_t \end{pmatrix} A\varepsilon_t = \begin{pmatrix} 1 & 0 & 0 & 0 & 0 \\ a_{21} & 1 & 0 & 0 & 0 \\ a_{31} & a_{32} & 1 & 0 & 0 \\ a_{41} & a_{42} & a_{43} & 1 & 0 \\ a_{51} & a_{52} & a_{53} & a_{54} & 1 \end{pmatrix} \begin{pmatrix} \varepsilon_{g_t} \\ \varepsilon_{x_t} \\ \varepsilon_{\pi_t} \\ \varepsilon_{r_t} \\ \varepsilon_{i_t} \end{pmatrix}.$$

Furthermore, vector y_t represents all the model equations or specifications for each used variable, vector b_0 represents the constants of all the equations, and vector ε_t represents the error components.

In addition, the causalities in the structural models are identified by using the most commonly used technique based on contemporary (short-term) restrictions—Cholesky factorisation. In other words, it imposes a particular causal chain and identifies the system recursively. The used models are built under the assumption that government expenditure gap is strictly exogenous, meaning that it is not influenced by the other variables. Hence, it is ordered first, even before the output gap. According to Ilzetzki et al. (2011), it is reasonable to assume that the output gap reacts to changes in government expenditure gap immediately. However, government expenditure usually does not immediately react to a shock from the output. The fact is that because of the existence of various fiscal policies and data lags.

Furthermore, the third variable is the inflation rate, which is directly influenced by government expenditure and output gaps. Finally, the last two variables are government revenue and monetary policy-relevant interest rate. The interest rate is ordered last, meaning it is considered strictly endogenous, which is a reasonable assumption given the monetary policy determinants. Furthermore, the interest rate does not affect any other variable in the short term, which is in accordance with monetary policy lags.[16]

I use one of the most commonly used estimation approaches, developed by Litterman (1986), denoted as the Minnesota prior. The estimation procedure considers a normal prior on a set of parameters with the fixed and known residual covariance matrix. However, I do not use the original Litterman's

(continued)

[16] I refer to the Monetary Transmission Mechanism. The pass-through from short-term interest rate to the main macroeconomic variables usually takes some time.

Box 8.2 (continued)
restricted diagonal matrix and replace it with a full-VAR matrix estimated by OLS to incorporate more information. Hence, only the vector of parameters is unknown. The Minnesota prior imposes a hypothesis that the variables follow a random walk process. In addition, I estimated and optimised the values of prior hyperparameters within the Bayesian framework using a grid search introduced by Giannone et al. (2012). The estimated coefficients maximise the value of the marginal likelihoods of the models. The procedure finds the corresponding values based on a specified interval of minimum and maximum (plausible) values for each hyperparameter. Therefore, the prior coefficients are not biased by subjective opinion and are set individually for all the estimated models. The estimations were performed using a MATLAB toolbox developed by Dieppe et al. (2016) within the ECB. It should be noted that relevant statistical tests were conducted, and the presented models suffice the VAR stability condition.

The presented models cannot reflect the structural changes that occurred in the EU4 countries. Therefore, I split each country estimate into separate time periods, and the years during which the countries showed recessions occur are not included. The time frames were selected to be consistent with the previous estimates in this work and to reflect the development of real GDP growth rates.[17] Table 8.2 presents the main results—the values of cumulative impulse-response functions (expenditure multipliers) for 20 quarters ahead because it is not feasible to assume further impact. The assumption is in accordance with the empirical literature.

Nevertheless, I must note that the IRFs are persistent in some cases and do not completely fade out within 20 quarters. Furthermore, the results are contrasted with estimations obtained using the same methodology on the pre-COVID-19 crisis data—the period of 2000–2019. In some cases, the COVID-19 crisis has introduced a significant structural shock along with large revisions of gap components. Hence, the estimations are different. As it was noted, the result should be treated with caution.

Note that the estimates for the total period (which was structurally unstable) show negative values of expenditure multipliers. The results can be interpreted that an increase in government expenditure above some sustainable level led to a net decrease in GDP.[18] The result corroborates the research of Ilzetzki et al. (2011). Nevertheless, it can be a result of various aspects. First, the period showed significant structural changes (the financial crisis of 2008–2009 and the COVID-19 crisis,

[17]The recession did not begin in the same quarter in the case of all the countries. However, the common time frame is used for simplicity and comparability of the estimates in time. However, the differences are negligible.

[18]The estimations work with GDP gaps, as was mentioned; however, I use the term GDP solely for better interpretation and easier understanding of the conclusions.

Table 8.2 Country-specific estimates of cumulative expenditure multipliers (5 years ahead)—EU4, selected periods of 2000–2021

Country	Total period[a] (2000–2021)	Pre-financial-crisis period (2000–2008)	Pre-COVID-19 crisis period (2014–2019)
Italy	−2.1 (−0.6)	0.4 (0.3)	0.1 (1.4)
Spain	−2.8 (−4.0)	0.3 (0.3)	2.3 (0.7)
Portugal	−0.2 (−0.3)	0.8 (0.3)	1.3 (1.4)
Greece	−0.4 (−1.8)	0.1 (0.0)	4.1 (1.3)

Notes: Pre-COVID-19 estimates (2000–2019) are included in parentheses. The total period pre-COVID-19 estimates reflect the time frame of 2000–2019 instead of 2000–2021. The data were rounded to one decimal point

Source: Own calculations and processing

[a]The results should be treated with caution. Structural breaks and data revision effects are significant

which began in 2020). Second, this may result from unsustainable and harmful government policies systematically stimulating the economies and deepening economic inefficiencies. For instance, the countries' competitiveness and motivation to work were significantly lowered. Moreover, many job positions and even businesses, which would be unprofitable under normal circumstances, were kept alive.

The pre-financial-crisis period was characterised by immensely low multipliers of approximately 0.1–0.8. The evidence suggests that each euro of government expenditure generated only 0.1–0.8 euros of total output or GDP. It means that the fiscal policy efforts were highly inefficient and were wasting resources as a significant crowding-out effect of private investment occurred. In other words, the resources could have been put to better use if they were not redistributed and used by the public sector.[19]

The estimates suggest that the values of the multipliers in the pre-COVID-19 crisis period were significantly larger, even higher than one, for all the countries except Italy.[20] The increase in multipliers corresponds with the economic theory. Nevertheless, the development needs to be put into context. The countries had experienced a period of negative output gaps even in the post-recession period.[21] Furthermore, they were arguably less 'overheated' in the subsequent years when compared to the period before the financial crisis. It is consistent with the previous estimates of the output gaps. Therefore, the values of fiscal multipliers were expected to be higher. Most countries were in a position where 1 euro of government expenditure was able to increase total output by more than 1, as suggested by the estimates.

[19] I do not claim that all government expenditures are inefficient. The sector may be able to enhance allocation efficiency in many cases, for instance, by long-term investment in infrastructure, digitalisation, or education.

[20] Moreover, the multiplier of 4.1 regarding Greece is rather high. It may reflect potential issues with the stability of the examined variables in the relevant time frame in Greece.

[21] Refer to the sixth chapter.

Nevertheless, it does not mean that increases in government expenditure would solve the issues of the EU4 countries. It was a temporary phenomenon. It suggests that fiscal austerity without structural reforms is probably unsuitable for EU4 countries.[22]

References

Afonso, A., & Leal, F. S. (2019). Fiscal multipliers in the Eurozone: A SVAR analysis. *Applied Economics, 51*(51), 5577–5593. https://doi.org/10.1080/00036846.2019.1616068

Amendola, A., et al. (2019). *The Euro-Area government spending multiplier at the effective lower bound* (IMF Working Paper No. 19/133). International Monetary Fund. Retrieved August 2, 2022, from https://www.imf.org/en/Publications/WP/Issues/2019/06/28/The-Euro-Area-Government-Spending-Multiplier-at-the-Effective-Lower-Bound-46896

Banerjee, A., Dolado, J., & Mestre, R. (1998). Error-correction mechanism tests for cointegration in a single-equation framework. *Journal of Time Series Analysis, 19*(3), 267–283. https://doi.org/10.1111/1467-9892.00091

Batini, N., et al. (2014). *Fiscal multipliers: Size, determinants, and use in macroeconomic projections* (Technical Note and Manual No. 2014/04). International Monetary Fund. Retrieved August 2, 2022, from https://www.imf.org/en/Publications/TNM/Issues/2016/12/31/Fiscal-Multipliers-Size-Determinants-and-Use-in-Macroeconomic-Projections-41784

Berti, K., et al. (2016). *Fiscal reaction functions for European Union countries* (Discussion Paper 028 (April 2016)). European Commission. Retrieved July 3, 2022, from https://ec.europa.eu/info/sites/info/files/dp028_en.pdf

Blanchard, O., & Perotti, R. (2002). An empirical characterization of the dynamic effects of changes in government spending and taxes on output. *The Quarterly Journal of Economics, 117*(4), 1329–1368. http://www.jstor.org/stable/4132480

Bohn, H. (1998). The behavior of U.S. public debt and deficits. *The Quarterly Journal of Economics, 113*(3), 949–963. https://doi.org/10.2307/2586878

Burger, P., et al. (2011). *Fiscal sustainability and the fiscal reaction function for South Africa* (IMF Working Paper No. 11/69). International Monetary Fund. Retrieved July 3, 2022, from https://www.imf.org/external/pubs/ft/wp/2011/wp1169.pdf

Caldara, D., & Kamps, C. (2008). *What are the effects of fiscal policy shocks? A VAR-based comparative analysis* (ECB Working Paper No. 877). European Central Bank. Retrieved July 26, 2022, from https://www.ecb.europa.eu/pub/pdf/scpwps/ecbwp877.pdf

Clark, P. K. (1987). The cyclical component of U. S. economic activity. *The Quarterly Journal of Economics, 102*(4), 797–814. https://doi.org/10.2307/1884282

Dieppe, A., Legrand, R., & van Roye, B. (2016). *The BEAR toolbox* (ECB Working Paper No. 1934). European Central Bank. Retrieved July 26, 2022, from https://www.ecb.europa.eu/pub/pdf/scpwps/ecbwp1934.en.pdf

Eurostat. (2022). *Eurostat database*. Retrieved September 21, 2022, from https://ec.europa.eu/eurostat

Federal Reserve Bank of St. Louis (St. Louis Fed). (2022). *Federal Reserve Economic Data* (FRED Database). Retrieved April 11, 2022, from https://fred.stlouisfed.org/

[22] Appropriate structural reforms could further improve allocation efficiency. For instance, they may include structural deregulations or establishing individual currencies, which would mean leaving the Euro Area.

Giannone, D., Lenza, M., & Primiceri, G. (2012). *Prior selection for vector autoregressions* (ECARES Working Paper 2012-002). ULB – Universite Libre de Bruxelles. https://EconPapers.repec.org/RePEc:eca:wpaper:2013/106648

Grant, A. L., & Chan, J. C. C. (2017). *Measuring the output gap using stochastic model specification search* (Working Paper). Retrieved March 15, 2022, from https://joshuachan.org/papers/output-gap-SMSS.pdf

Hall, R. (2009). *By how much does GDP rise if the government buys more output?* (NBER Working Paper No. 15496). National Bureau of Economic Research. https://doi.org/10.3386/w15496

Harvey, A. C. (1985). Trends and cycles in macroeconomic time series. *Journal of Business & Economic Statistics, 3*(3), 216–227. https://doi.org/10.1080/07350015.1985.10509453

Ilzetzki, E., Mendoza, E. G., & Végh, C. A. (2011). *How big (small?) are fiscal multipliers?* (IMF Working Paper No. 11/52). International Monetary Fund. Retrieved July 26, 2022, from https://www.imf.org/external/pubs/ft/wp/2011/wp1152.pdf

International Monetary Fund (IMF). (2022). *Public finances in modern history dataset*. Retrieved August 15, 2022, from https://www.imf.org/external/datamapper/datasets/FPP

Kempa, B., & Khan, N. S. (2015). On the size of government spending multipliers in Europe. *Applied Economics, 47*(51), 5548–5558. https://doi.org/10.1080/00036846.2015.1054067

Kilian, L., & Lütkepohl, H. (2017). *Structural vector autoregressive analysis*. Cambridge University Press.. https://doi.org/10.1017/9781108164818. ISBN: 978-11-08-16481-8.

Legrenzi, G., & Milas, C. (2013). *Modelling the fiscal reaction functions of the GIPS based on state-varying thresholds* (CESIFO Working Paper No. 4385). Center for Economic Studies & Ifo Institute. Retrieved July 3, 2022, from https://www.cesifo.org/DocDL/cesifo1_wp4385.pdf

Litterman, R. B. (1986). Forecasting with Bayesian vector autoregressions—five years of experience. *Journal of Business & Economic Statistics, 4*(1), 25–38. https://doi.org/10.1080/07350015.1986.10509491

Miyamoto, W., Nguyen, T. L., & Sergeyev, D. (2018). Government spending multipliers under the zero lower bound: Evidence from Japan. *American Economic Journal: Macroeconomics, 10*(3), 247–277. https://doi.org/10.1257/mac.20170131

Senekovič, M., Kavkler, A., & Bekő, J. (2019). Estimation of government spending multiplier in EU economies. *Naše gospodarstvo / Our economy, 65*(1), 16–29. https://doi.org/10.2478/ngoe-2019-0002

Shiller, R. (2022). *Online data*. Retrieved June 14, 2022, from http://www.econ.yale.edu/~shiller/data.htm

Warmedinger, T., Checherita-Westphal, C., & de Cos, P. H. (2015). *What are the effects of fiscal policy shocks? A VAR-based comparative analysis* (Occasional Paper Series No. 162). European Central Bank. Retrieved August 2, 2022, from https://www.ecb.europa.eu/pub/pdf/scpops/ecbop162.en.pdf

Chapter 9
Sovereign Debt Resolution Prospects

The chapter puts together the previous text and analyses the possibilities of dealing with the excessive indebtedness of the EU4 countries. Its objective is to provide an overview of suitable options and objectively analyse the position of the EU4 countries. It should be noted that it is primarily examining mid-term and long-term outlooks and resolutions as opposed to short-term perspectives, which EU officials often emphasise. Furthermore, it addresses various counterarguments and identifies false arguments.

The structure of the chapter follows the main categories of options regarding debt reduction. There are three ways how to raise additional resources to fund a budget deficit: debt financing (domestic or external debt), money financed deficit (debt monetisation), and sale of assets (Strecha, 2015). These options can also be useful when trying to reduce indebtedness. Debt monetisation can help finance the debt and the sale of assets. Other, more general ways of reducing relative indebtedness include a change in fiscal policy stance (fiscal consolidation—increasing revenues or decreasing expenditures), sovereign default, or reliance on GDP growth. Finally, the last section provides a summary and recommendations regarding the most suitable scenario.

9.1 Debt Monetisation in the Euro Area

Monetisation can help reduce indebtedness in two ways. First, if a bail-out takes place, government debt is repaid by other subjects. Second, inflationary pressures reduce the real value of debt stock. However, the issue of debt monetisation is more complicated when it is conducted in a monetary union, and it needs to be analysed separately. Problems in Europe, which started during the first half of the 1990s, strengthened the drive for the Economic and Monetary Union of the EU (Gros, 2012). Back then, it was argued, by Spain and Italy, that the only way out of the

M. Bednář, *Fiscal Policy in the Southern European Union Countries*, Contributions to Finance and Accounting, https://doi.org/10.1007/978-3-031-29761-8_9

inflation and continuous depreciation was joining the Euro Area. Nevertheless, the Euro Area crisis leads to the opposite conclusions (ibid.).

According to Gros (2012, p. 36): 'It is now argued that financing a high public debt in a monetary union is particularly difficult, or at least unstable, because a government that loses the confidence of investors has no other option left than to default'. Arguably, this fact led to strengthening the socialisation of risks in the Euro Area. In addition, a monetary union is usually undergoing some phases, and once the Euro Area's initial phase with its low-interest levels and high growth rates expires, it will become even more challenging to reduce the indebtedness of the countries (Baumgarten & Klodt, 2010). Arguably, the Euro Area is currently experiencing the next phase of low growth.

The flaws of the monetary union have already been analysed in the previous chapters. Nevertheless, some of the relevant issues should be briefly mentioned. Sinn (2018) discusses interest rate and exchange rate blockage, comparing the situation to the case of Dutch disease, which is hampering the competitiveness of the EU4 countries. Moreover, the current state of TARGET2 imbalances is another possible indicator of the situation. The imbalances got much higher than their financial crisis peak levels around 2012, and they currently amount to double-digit shares of GDP in the case of the EU4 countries (Eurostat, 2022). If the monetary union functioned well, there would be no significant imbalances as the created liquidity would be absorbed by the countries' banking systems more evenly. These facts show that debt monetisation is even more problematic in the Euro Area compared to a standard 'isolated' one-country approach.

It should be added that membership in the Euro Area implies that ECB needs to make a final decision about debt monetisation, not the individual central banks of the member countries. Lucarelli (2011) claims that national governments need to rely more on financial markets in the formulation of national policies, which is sub-optimal. In other words, the ECB is in a desperate position due to the structural faults of the Euro Area. The current data showed that even before the COVID-19 crisis, the risk perceptions and fragmentation of the Euro Area did not disappear (see Eurostat, 2022). The risk of additional bail-outs in the Euro Area was still in play, and it materialised in the COVID-19 aftermath in the form of a stronger risk-sharing.[1] A bail-out or stronger-risk sharing mechanisms are not sustainable or desirable, especially if no significant changes to the system are made.[2]

In the past, quantitative easing did not arguably exhibit significant inflationary pressures. Hence, many economists were finding relevant arguments and arguably underestimated this phenomenon. Nevertheless, the combination of quantitative easing with the COVID-19 crisis and strong fiscal impulses after 2019 showed how impactful and unstable this policy strategy is.[3] Inflationary pressures could

[1] I refer to the Next Generation EU package and the issuance of common EU bonds.

[2] Refer to the discussion about the changes in the composition of the Euro Area in the third chapter.

[3] Currently, major central banks are discussing or slowly entering the policy of quantitative tightening.

absorb another portion of the debt; however, it affects the whole economy, creating instabilities and uncertainty, and there is no particular reason why debtors should benefit at the expense of creditors. Moreover, some of the effects are hidden. Real estate markets are booming in many countries, and prices or yields of government bonds are also affected. While the latter leads to easier debt management, it is possibly causing relative losses for subjects holding these instruments due to market distortions such as pension funds. Furthermore, the governments experience no direct feedback that would arise from their expansionary policies.[4]

The current expansionary strategies of many central banks undoubtedly helped in the short term, most notably during the crisis periods. However, continuing the trend is a fatal mistake because it will worsen the situation. Quantitative easing cannot solve the structural issues of low inflation and low GDP growth; it creates new issues. According to Lucarelli (2011, p. 213): '*The imposition of a one size fits all monetary policy by the ECB has only exacerbated asymmetries between the low-inflation and high-inflation countries*'. Arguably, due to political motivations, there is a lack of emphasis on real competitive advantages[5] compared to the past. The current expansionary monetary policy of the ECB is like trying to start a broken engine by kicking it. Therefore, solving the indebtedness using mainly money financing in the Euro Area is not an appropriate solution.

Arguably, the current situation was caused by political decisions that seem to be trapped in a false ideology or a sunk cost fallacy. The idea of '*buying time*' before some significant changes are made is not very convincing either, as there are no guarantees, and it paradoxically helps sustain the current status quo. Baltatescu (2013) argues that even if a fiscal union is set up, there are no reasons to believe that the debt problem of the Euro Area will be solved, provided that the socialisation of risks and losses across the region remains possible. The issue was analysed in the fifth chapter. A slightly better solution is to decrease the real value of debt by inflationary pressures within a separate domestic currency (which would mean that the EU4 countries need to leave the Euro Area). However, as mentioned, the option is inefficient and dangerous when considering its other effects.

9.2 Fiscal Consolidation

Fiscal consolidation refers to a broad spectrum of financial adjustment aimed at strengthening of the fiscal and debt position of a country. In theory, we distinguish between short-term and long-term measures. Hence, all the approaches are analysed and put into the relevant context of the EU4 countries in the following text.

---

[4]Refer to the blockage of interest rate pass-through presented in Chap. 3.

[5]It refers to those competitive advantages that were created on the basis of market-led economic productivity.

Table 9.1 General government gross financial assets, GDP ratios—EU4, selected years of 2000–2021

Year	Italy	Spain	Portugal	Greece
2000	24.7%	23.2%	23.7%	28.5%
2005	25.1%	22.5%	24.5%	33.3%
2010	25.7%	28.8%	33.4%	37.6%
2015	29%	37.1%	41.6%	43.1%
2019	29.5%	34.3%	36.9%	57.9%
2020	33.2%	40.2%	44.8%	61.5%
2021	N/A[a]	40.9%	40.1%	57.8%

Source: Eurostat (2022), own processing
[a]Data are unavailable as of 3Q 2022

9.2.1 Temporary Measures: Sales of Assets

When a country is pushed into selling its assets, there exists an opportunistic behaviour of subjects that are willing to buy them. It has nothing to do with an optimal strategy for such country, and it will arguably hurt the economy in most cases. However, selling the assets may offer a temporary solution to a government debt reduction. Therefore, we analyse general government gross financial assets individually, assuming they could be sold.[6] The respective values for the EU4 countries are presented in Table 9.1.

The data show that even under the assumption of selling all these assets, none of the countries could reduce its indebtedness ratio below 60% of GDP. Nevertheless, it is almost certain that some assets are of low performance or even illiquid; thus, they cannot be easily sold. Moreover, a sale of performing assets would mean higher debt inertia from a long-term perspective. Finally, selling certain short-term instruments could disrupt the country's budget management. Therefore, the strategy of an asset sale is not feasible.

9.2.2 Long-Term Measures: Revenues and Expenditures

The depth of a reduction of indebtedness depends on how efficient a fiscal consolidation is. In other words, it depends on which tools are used and how strictly and fast they are implemented. From the theoretical perspective, even a short-term increase in government debt may help boost growth and lower relative indebtedness. The assumption of making credible investments is, however, often not fulfilled.

While the opinions on fiscal consolidation in the relevant literature are mixed, no other tools for reducing indebtedness are left besides GDP growth and sovereign default. The EU experienced some historical events of sizeable reductions in debt

[6]There is a lack of detailed data on general government non-financial assets. Nevertheless, these assets are usually made mostly of buildings and natural resources. Most of them are arguably not fit to be sold under standard circumstances.

ratios. For instance, 50 percentage points in Belgium from 1994 to 2007, and more than 69 percentage points in Ireland from 1994 to 2006 (ECB, 2010).

On the one hand, Cafiso and Cellini (2014) claim that fiscal consolidations are inefficient in reducing relative indebtedness. Jeong (2017) reached the same conclusion. On the other hand, it can be theoretically argued that fiscal consolidations can help countries escape a bad or unsustainable equilibrium (Padoani et al., 2012). Such programmes may boost market confidence and lower risk premia over an extended period. Fiscal consolidation may initially depress economic growth, but arguably not to the extent that it would push a country into a bad equilibrium or prevent it from escaping (ibid.). According to Cottarelli et al. (2014), history shows several episodes of fiscal adjustments that were characterised by medium-term sustainable growth. The growth is needed to ensure that the country is not losing its international competitiveness while it supports further debt reduction. Historical experience demonstrates that drastic consolidation measures will face massive political resistance and a sharp increase in unemployment (Baumgarten & Klodt, 2010). A gradual adjustment would be the most suitable pace of consolidation.

Two possible ways of balancing a budget are increasing revenues or cutting expenditures. Theoretically, raising taxes (increasing revenues) is problematic as it dampens individual motivations to work, raises costs, and reduces the country's competitiveness.[7] Eventually, it constricts economic growth and lowers potential GDP. Attinasi and Metelli (2016) argue that when fiscal consolidation is based on an increase in government revenues, the initial increase in the debt ratio is more potent, and eventually, the debt ratio reverts to its pre-shock level. It results in the so-called *self-defeating austerity*. Even critics of fiscal consolidations, Cafiso and Cellini (2014), recommend that such measures should be based on savings or cutting costs because fiscal consolidations made by an increase in taxation are more likely to have adverse medium-term effects. According to Eurostat (2022), Italy and Greece ranked among the top 10 EU countries with the highest tax wedge. Portugal and Spain are performing relatively better, but the differences between EU19 and EU28 are relatively small. To conclude, efficient fiscal consolidations should be gradual and credible, and they should focus on cutting public expenditures.

9.2.3 Long-Term Measures: Administrative Tools

Forms of administrative measures—various fiscal rules, seem inefficient from a theoretical perspective when they are used as the primary tool for preventing debt accumulation. Such measures are, in principle, tools of central economic planning. The situation is worse considering that these rules are also imposed on sovereign countries, which is why these rules are mostly recommendations on a supranational level. Evidently, the main impulses must come from within the economy, not as a

[7] Especially in the case of already high tax revenue to GDP ratios (tax quota or tax wedge).

purely external factor. Of course, politicians agreed to follow such measures; however, their pledge in the case of the EU was arguably rather populistic.[8] Another piece of evidence may be provided by the public, as many individuals do not know that such measures even exist. It demonstrates that fiscal rules are often completely disconnected from the political process. Hence, their enforceability and motivations to follow them are low.

The efficiency of administrative measures highly depends on the individual country and its position in time. Furthermore, when administrative rules are applied, the country is already facing problems in many cases. Therefore, it is highly problematic to empirically measure the effect of imposed fiscal rules (a problem of endogeneity). Heinemann et al. (2018) used a meta-regression analysis based on 30 studies published in the last decade. They found positive effects of these rules. Nevertheless, the authors added that their results might be biased due to potential endogeneity issues. In addition, the authors found a presence of publication bias. It may be beneficial to develop other strategies, such as establishing independent fiscal boards or the role of disciplining incentives from bond markets (ibid.). However, politicians do not comply in many cases because the fiscal boards provide only recommendations that cannot be enforced. In addition, the role of disciplining incentives is deficient, and improvement is impossible because of the ECB's quantitative easing programmes.[9] The current EU and Euro area administrative measures are rather 'cosmetic' or populistic. Arguably, they are not able to make a fundamental difference.

9.3 Structural Reforms Promoting Economic Growth

Reforms focusing on the economic structure and promoting economic growth are possibly one of the most efficient approaches. It helps in three ways. First, government budget may be financed by raising revenues due to the expanding economy. Second, if the absolute value of accumulated debt does not change, higher GDP means a lower debt-to-GDP ratio. Third, harsh austerity measures may eventually lead to social unrest (Sarcinelli, 2012). Positive GDP growth can reduce the possibility significantly.

The current pace of economic growth in the Euro Area is unfortunately very low. The monetary union is among the slowest-growing regions in the world (see IMF, 2022).

Table 9.2 shows historical averages of the real GDP growth of the countries. Until 2020, the most problematic countries were Italy and Greece. Surprisingly, Italy

[8] Supranational fiscal regulations in the EU were breached several times in history, even by the EU itself during the financial crisis of 2008–2009. Moreover, even national fiscal rules were breached in history as the legislation can be flexibly amended.

[9] The consequences of the expansive monetary policy were already mentioned in previous chapters.

Table 9.2 Real GDP growth rates, geometric averages—EU4, selected periods of 2000–2021

Country	Total period (2000–2021)	Pre-financial-crisis period (2000–2008)	Financial crisis period (2009–2013)	Post-recession period (2014–2019)	Coronavirus crisis period (2020–2021)
Italy	0.22%	1.18%	−1.57%	0.87%	−1.51%
Spain	1.36%	3.35%	−1.77%	2.60%	−3.18%
Portugal	0.62%	1.39%	−1.64%	2.26%	−1.98%
Greece	0.17%	3.55%	−5.94%	0.73%	−0.73%
EU27	1.37%	2.17%	−0.23%	2.10%	−0.41%
EU19[a]	1.16%	1.95%	−0.39%	1.88%	−0.67%

Source: Eurostat (2022), own processing
[a]Data are based on the changing composition of the Euro Area

Table 9.3 Number of episodes when GDP growth was the dominant factor of relative general government gross debt to GDP reductions—EU4, 2000–2021

Italy	Spain	Portugal	Greece
1 of the last 22 years	6 of the last 22 years	5 of the last 22 years	3 of the last 22 years

Note: The values are based on the debt dynamics presented in the seventh chapter
Source: Own calculations and processing

showed slower average growth than Greece in the post-recession period. Moreover, notice how the EU4 shows considerably higher economic decline in the recession periods and not significantly higher growth rates in the recovery periods compared to the EU27 or the Euro Area aggregates.

Possibly, more precise information is obtained from the decomposition of debt dynamics—the effects of GDP growth are presented in Table 9.3. For the given period, not a single examined country achieved that GDP growth was the main factor of change in indebtedness for at least 40% of the time.[10] Therefore, there may exist a significant opportunity gap. Such a transition would, however, need a significant political change in the EU and the Euro Area, which may not be politically feasible.

A crucial question when solving debt issues is 'how the growth would be created and whether it is sustainable or not'. Do the current monetary and fiscal policies in the Euro Area create such growth? Evidently not, although policymakers often argue the positive effects of economic growth. Sustainable and robust economic development can be created by boosting competitive advantages. First, a change of monetary policy conduct is needed to stop giving governments incentives to accumulate debts by reducing sovereign bond interest rates.[11] Second, it would mean a change in the Euro Area's design and structure—exit of some countries or annulment of

[10]Nevertheless, primary balances, which are connected to GDP growth rates to some extent, were often the deciding factor.

[11]The problem is complex. Interest rate reduction may serve as a beneficial factor; however, as was stated in the third chapter, the current monetary policy in the Euro Area has adverse effects. Hence, policy advocates are frequently using false argumentation.

Table 9.4 Length of sovereign defaults (for both domestic and external debt)—EU4, 1820–2021

Italy	Spain	Portugal	Greece
7 years	47 years	24 years	120 years

Source: Bank of Canada and Bank of England (2022) and Reinhart (2010), own calculations and processing

socialisation of risks and losses in the EU or the Euro Area (as stated by Baltatescu, 2013). The problem is that the EU is trying to deal with many issues while promoting unstable and non-functional political integration. Third, the relevant countries need to cut the size of their public sectors; a snowball effect has occurred for decades.[12] Fourth, the bureaucracy and tax burden imposed on the private sector should be mitigated. Finally, I recommend making efficient investments in education[13] and research and development.

To conclude, a return to market principles is needed in many cases. If there is no major reform, many EU countries should expect prolonged years of weak economic growth or stagnation while increasing the debt burden simultaneously. The EU4 countries will be in the worst position in such a case.

9.4 Government Default

When a country cannot fully repay its debt, a government default occurs. The cases of sovereign defaults should be treated individually, as they may significantly differ. Especially defaults in a monetary union should be scrutinised. The consequences of a sovereign default are quite straightforward. The lender entity loses its resources, while the debtor country (and its citizens) face possible consequences in terms of reputation costs, possible sanctions, or economic, political, and social crises. Nevertheless, the implications of sovereign indebtedness differ from private indebtedness (Borensztein & Panizza, 2008). In the former case, the creditors have an arguably weaker position than in the case of private debts. Further, the legal rights of repayments are, in fact, limited because of the sovereignty of the debtor country (ibid.).

Table 9.4 draws from the history of more than 200 years of sovereign defaults. Unfortunately, these events are not rare. Greece, Spain, and Portugal experienced many episodes of default in history. Moreover, Greece spent more than half of the selected period in default, with the longest episode lasting for 33 years (1932–1964). In addition, the countries usually defaulted based on foreign debt. The current

[12]For example, see the data of OECD (2022).

[13]A proper state of education, connected to critical thinking, is able to solve many issues, including those resulting from a political process.

situation is no exception; however, the use of the common euro currency makes the situation less transparent.[14]

The literature offers some historical insights into the costs of sovereign defaults. It agrees that a default event means high costs for the debtor country, although there is some evidence that the long-lasting effects are not always present. Baer et al. (2011) analysed the default of Argentina in 2001. They concluded that it was accompanied by a catastrophic economic, political, and social crisis that reduced the country's significance and made multilateral institutions more sympathetic. Arguably, the EU4 countries are in a similar situation. Borensztein and Panizza (2008) list four types of costs that may result from an international sovereign default: reputational costs, international trade exclusion, costs incurred to the domestic economy through the financial system, and political costs. They found that the costs are generally high (but short-lived), especially political costs.

Gros and Mayer (2011) mention possible problems connected to the '*debt restructuring*' in the case of Greece. It may be too costly and is no substitute for the required economic adjustment. Countries in a similar situation may lose their access to financial markets. Moreover, debt restructuring will create moral hazards, which could lead to a broader crisis.

On the one hand, another series of significant defaults in the Euro Area would mean making it (or the whole EU) even less economically efficient than it currently is and possibly fostering or creating new structural problems. On the other hand, a government default is arguably needed in extreme cases to set a country on the '*right*' track again (Gros & Mayer, 2011). The authors add that lenders should be punished for lending to these countries.

Some economists (for example, Skaperdas, 2015) claim that the interests of government officials and the interests of the country are different; therefore, individuals should not be punished. The institute of democracy is not perfect; however, the argument is invalid because there would be a lack of responsibility for elections, which would further impede the efficiency of the political process. The default argument seems convincing even though most of these lenders are EU citizens. According to Skaperdas (2015, p. 758): '*If the lender has not been careful in choosing his borrowers, then it is both economically efficient and fair that he loses. From an economic viewpoint, it is clear that the possibility of bankruptcy has been a usual source of improvement, renewal, and vitality in the economies that allow it*'. Nevertheless, a particular cause of de facto bankruptcy in Greece needs to be addressed. From both empirical and theoretical perspectives, such a significant event as the government default needs to be executed properly. Half-done policies, especially when facing a severe crisis, are usually not successful. In other words, bailed-out bankruptcy, which preserves the current status-quo, does not bear the desired effects.

[14]Common currency serves as a '*shield*' against adverse exchange rate fluctuations, but it does not fully mitigate the pressures from non-resident countries which share the currency.

Evidently, a sovereign default should be an option of last resort. The question is whether the Euro Area is in such a desperate situation. Skaperdas (2015) claims that an event of default may not necessarily be as disastrous as it is often presented. Without the euro, it is difficult to imagine how a crisis of such depth would have occurred (ibid.). Furthermore, as was shown in the previous chapters, if no structural reforms take place, the EU4 countries are caught in a debt trap that could lead to a dangerous spiral of debt increase while experiencing economic stagnation. If the current status quo is being preserved, it seems fit for these countries to default. It would help shape voters' demands, thus helping the political process (the subjects involved would face immediate consequences). Subsequently, it would accelerate the reform of the EU's and the Euro Area's structural weaknesses and discard unreasonable policies. In other words, defaults would accelerate the functioning of correction mechanisms (or help with their creation) in the Euro Area and the EU if there is no political will to do so.

9.5 Appropriate Solutions

The chapter identified and analysed four main possibilities for dealing with the debts: debt monetisation, fiscal consolidation, structural reforms, and sovereign default. As practised by the ECB, debt monetisation is not an appropriate solution. Its primary effects are based on a short-term perspective, while its secondary effects worsen the situation. The effects include the creation of further imbalances in the TARGET2 system, thus raising the probability of another bail-out. Moreover, the socialisation of risks and losses likely strengthens the moral hazard in the EU and the Euro Area. Additional inflationary pressures create other instabilities, and there is no particular reason why debtors should benefit at the expense of creditors. Additionally, some effects are hidden. Real estate markets in the countries are booming, and both prices and yields of government bonds are affected. The crucial aspect is that governments issuing financial instruments experience no relevant feedback that would arise from their expansionary policies.

The second possibility is fiscal consolidation which needs to be gradual and credible, and it should focus on cutting expenditures rather than increasing revenues by raising tax rates. However, the target is not achievable without structural reforms promoting economic growth. Arguably, there is an opportunity gap regarding higher GDP growth because the Euro Area is among the slowest growing regions in the world. Some authors claim that the reforms should be mainly demand-driven. Nevertheless, I demonstrated that this is not the case considering the previous analyses regarding the Euro Area's instabilities.

Finally, there is a lack of emphasis on real competitive advantages due to political motivations. In many cases, a return to market principles is needed. It contrasts with the usual short-term reforms focusing on the demand side of the economy. The structural reforms must include a return to country-specific currencies in the EU4 countries due to the systemic instabilities in the Euro Area. When there is an insufficient political will to conduct reforms, a proper and fully executed sovereign default will accelerate the functioning of correction mechanisms in the EU and the Euro Area. Unfortunately, such action was not executed in the case of Greece, even though the country was de facto bankrupted.

References

Attinasi, M. G., & Metelli, L. (2016). *Is fiscal consolidation self-defeating? A panel-Var analysis for the Euro Area countries* (ECB Working Paper No. 1883). European Central Bank. Retrieved July 16, 2022, from https://www.ecb.europa.eu/pub/pdf/scpwps/ecbwp1883.en.pdf

Baer, W., Margot, D., & Montes-Rojas, G. (2011). Argentina's default and the lack of dire consequences. *Economia Aplicada, 15*, 131–146. http://www.scielo.br/scielo.php?script=sci_arttext&pid=S1413-80502011000100007&nrm=iso

Baltatescu, I. (2013). Eurozone public debt problem: An analysis from the perspective of the institutions and policies. *Global Economic Observer, 1*(1), 83–92. https://ideas.repec.org/a/ntu/ntugeo/vol1-iss1-13-083.html

Bank of Canada and Bank of England. (2022). *CRAG Database 2021*. Retrieved August 16, 2022, from https://www.bankofcanada.ca/wp-content/uploads/2021/06/CRAG-Database-Update-05-07-21.xlsx

Baumgarten, M., & Klodt, H. (2010). Greece and beyond: The debt mechanics of the Euro. *Aussenwirtschaft, 65*(4), 365–377. http://ux-tauri.unisg.ch/RePEc/usg/auswrt/AW_65-0403_Baumgarten-Klodt.pdf

Borensztein, E., & Panizza, U. (2008). *The costs of sovereign default* (IMF Working Paper No. 08/238). International Monetary Fund. Retrieved July 16, 2022, from https://www.imf.org/en/Publications/WP/Issues/2016/12/31/The-Costs-of-Sovereign-Default-22346

Cafiso, G., & Cellini, R. (2014). Fiscal consolidations and public debt in Europe. *International Tax and Public Finance, 21*(4), 614–644. https://doi.org/10.1007/s10797-014-9319-y

Cottarelli, C., Gerson, P., & Senhadji, A. (2014). *Post-crisis fiscal policy*. The MIT Press. ISBN: 978-0262027182.

European Central Bank (ECB). (2010). *Monthly Bulletin (June 2010): Fiscal developments* (Monthly Bulletin No. 6/2010). Retrieved July 15, 2022, from https://www.ecb.europa.eu/pub/pdf/mobu/mb201006en.pdf

Eurostat. (2022). *Eurostat database*. Retrieved September 21, 2022, from https://ec.europa.eu/eurostat

Gros, D. (2012). On the stability of public debt in a monetary union. *JCMS: Journal of Common Market Studies, 50*, 36–48. https://doi.org/10.1111/j.1468-5965.2012.02273.x

Gros, D., & Mayer, T. (2011). To default or not to default? *CESifo Forum, 12*(2), 29–33. https://www.econstor.eu/handle/10419/166433

Heinemann, F., Moessinger, M.-D., & Yeter, M. (2018). Do fiscal rules constrain fiscal policy? A meta-regression-analysis. *European Journal of Political Economy, 51*, 69–92. https://doi.org/10.1016/j.ejpoleco.2017.03.008

International Monetary Fund (IMF). (2022). *World Economic Outlook Database*. Retrieved August 15, 2022, from https://www.imf.org/en/Publications/WEO

Jeong, K. J. (2017). Effects of fiscal consolidation in 18 OECD countries. *Seoul Journal of Economics, 30*(1), 51–91. https://ssrn.com/abstract=2925036

Lucarelli, B. (2011). German neomercantilism and the European sovereign debt crisis. *Journal of Post Keynesian Economics, 34*(2), 205–224. https://doi.org/10.2753/PKE0160-3477340202

Organisation for Economic Co-operation and Development (OECD). (2022). *Economic Outlook Database*. Retrieved August 20, 2022, from https://stats.oecd.org/

Padoani, P. C., Silai, U., & Noord, P. v. d. (2012). *Avoiding debt traps: Financial backstops and structural reforms* (OECD Economics Department Working Paper). Organisation for Economic Co-Operation and Development (OECD). https://doi.org/10.1787/5k962hhtt5mr-en

Reinhart, C. M. (2010). *This time is different chartbook: Country histories on debt, default, and financial crises* (NBER Working Paper No. 15815). National Bureau of Economic Research. https://doi.org/10.3386/w15815

Sarcinelli, M. (2012). Euro crisis or public debt crisis? With a remedy for the latter case. *PSL Quarterly Review, 65*(262), 215–236. https://ojs.uniroma1.it/index.php/PSLQuarterlyReview/article/view/10155

Sinn, H.-W. (2018). Brexit and the Euro crisis: What kind of union do we want? *Politická ekonomie, 66*(1), 3–19. https://doi.org/10.18267/j.polek.1174

Skaperdas, S. (2015). Myths and self-deceptions about the Greek debt crisis. *Revue d'Économie Politique, 125*(6), 755–785. https://doi.org/10.3917/redp.256.0755

Strecha, M. (2015). Public debt structure as an origin of economic instability. *Actual Problems in Economics, 2*(164), 328–338. https://bit.ly/2ZhVfaR

Chapter 10
Conclusions

This work focuses on analysing the fiscal policies of the EU4 countries (Italy, Spain, Portugal, and Greece) between 2000 and 2021. The EU4 countries form a relatively stable group (cluster) within the EU and the Euro Area. The most crucial distinction is the size of the economies. Smaller countries (Greece and Portugal) showed slightly different macroeconomic and fiscal behaviour than the larger countries (Italy and Spain).

According to the analyses, the general government debts of the EU4 countries are unsustainable in the medium- and long-term horizon. Furthermore, the current institutional design of the Euro Area is not suitable for the EU4 countries due to the existence of systemic flaws regarding the monetary union.

The EU4 countries suffer from a constant debt accumulation in the Euro Area. In particular, the monetary union is suffering from five main systemic flaws. These are overly ambitious integration ideology, the country composition of the Euro Area, socialisation of risks and moral hazard, dependence on the ECB, and snowball effects combined with systemic inertia. The Euro Area suffers from an overly ambitious integration ideology based on normative judgments rather than positive economic analysis. The ideology is deeply rooted in the political mainstream of Germany (and possibly France) and promotes sub-optimal policies for the EU4 countries.

Moreover, the EU4 economies are not functioning properly within the common currency system. An inflexible or relatively fixed exchange rate combined with the common monetary policy created a policy mix that promoted economic instabilities and motivated the EU4 countries to run unsustainable policies. The exchange rate channel is partly blocked as the common currency cannot properly depreciate and reflect the country's position. It led to lower GDP through the income channel, accompanied by higher debt pressures, internal devaluations, and capital outflows.

In addition, economic recovery mechanisms are also working inefficiently. The combination of previous factors promotes the widespread socialisation of risks and moral hazards. One of the main ideas is that the interest rate mechanism has also been blocked and cannot promote fiscal discipline. This factor, combined with the

M. Bednář, *Fiscal Policy in the Southern European Union Countries*, Contributions to Finance and Accounting, https://doi.org/10.1007/978-3-031-29761-8_10

short-term-oriented political processes, was able to preserve the sub-optimal status quo. Once individuals get used to a certain living standard, it is not politically feasible to deprive them of it. When the country's productivity does not cover such a living standard, it leads to high government deficits and further deterioration of the macroeconomic fundamentals. As a result, the EU4 countries gradually lose their national sovereignty and are increasingly dependent on centralised policy-making in the EU.

The common monetary policy of the ECB and its effects on the fiscal positions of the countries is complex and should be mentioned separately. An expansive monetary policy of the ECB leads to a temporary relaxation of fiscal conditions of the EU4 countries in the short term. However, it has significant adverse economic effects in the medium and long term. These include various market distortions such as bubbles in asset markets, prohibitive motivations, low fiscal discipline, and other factors. Paradoxically, the policy combined with the EU's mainstream political agenda led to unproductive investments, waste of resources, and the dependence of the EU4 countries on more fiscal stimuli.

Further, the common monetary policy of the ECB exacerbates the economic and structural inefficiencies in the Euro Area. Arguably, the current monetary policy of the ECB is a result of compromises within a heterogeneous group of countries. Moreover, the ECB is a fundamentally dependent central bank because the current Euro Area system needs constant interventions due to the fiscal dominance phenomenon. A significant increase in the ECB's key interest rate would result in another series of prohibitive debt accumulation of the EU4 countries associated with economic decline.

There exist eight sovereign debt channels in the Euro Area. They include institutional characteristics of the Euro Area, the nature of democracy and political cycles, information asymmetries, Keynesian stabilisation efforts, reputation and expectations, strict preferences, current economic conditions, and future prospects. The mechanisms fostered the indebtedness of the EU4 countries both directly and indirectly. The Euro Area does not form the optimum currency area, producing economic instabilities. The policymakers needed to promote unsustainable economic policies and introduce many compromise decisions within the institution to keep the common currency. This effect was further amplified by the political process, which is short-term oriented.

Furthermore, many politicians completely ignore the relevant structural problems of the Euro Area. They focused on Keynesian expansionary economic policies, which are not credible. In other words, they misinterpreted the occurrence and did not consider the structural flaws. This has led to a degradation of reputation and future expectations regarding the Euro Area countries. Nevertheless, the unsustainable fiscal policies of the EU4 countries cannot be attributed to external factors only. It could have been a result of strict preferences. A simple explanation is that individuals are willing to be better off in the short term at the expense of long-run problems because their life is finite, and they have a strong short-time preference. The current economic conditions of the EU4 countries are poor. This fact further contributes to a negative debt spiral. The EU4 countries will suffer from population ageing in the future. At the same time, there is competition between the '*old Western democracies*' and the rising superpowers such as China, which may put additional debt pressure. Finally, the EU4 countries were hit by the COVID-19 crisis in early 2020 and by the energy crisis associated with the Russian invasion of Ukraine.

Fiscal union is often mentioned as one of the possible solutions to the systemic instabilities of the Euro Area. Nevertheless, I identified eight main assumptions that would need to be met and concluded that there is not a single assumption that would not be seriously challenged. In fact, many of them would not be fulfilled. Establishing a fiscal union within the Euro Area would probably not be sustainable because a constant shift of resources from the Northern to the EU4 countries would need to occur. The fostered risk-sharing and the recent attempts to create a debt union in reaction to the COVID-19 crisis will ultimately lead to all the adverse effects we have seen in the recent past—during and after the financial crisis of 2008–2009.

The examined countries exhibited critical values of both flow and stock fiscal indicators between 2000 and 2021, with only a few exceptions. A more precise estimation of structural budget balances, which show '*true*' fiscal efforts, is problematic. Arguably, the European Commission's output gap estimates are not fully consistent with the macroeconomic behaviour of the countries within the Euro Area. Nevertheless, the EU4 countries destabilised their economies through prohibitive structural budget deficits. The values of the deficits were extremely high in Greece and Spain. They even outmatched the size of the GDP gaps at their peaks before the financial crisis.

Moreover, the analysis of debt dynamics indicated that automatic debt dynamics was crucial for Italy, Portugal, and Greece. The debt accumulation in Spain was highly determined by primary budget balances. It implies that this country has a larger '*manoeuvring*' space or higher potential for discretionary fiscal measures. In addition, the euro exchange rate fluctuations are not a problem per se due to negligible shares of debts denominated in foreign currencies in the EU4 countries.

Under the assumption that the EU4 countries would record average values of 2000–2021 of relevant debt drivers in the future, the debt development outlook for the EU4 countries is alarming. By 2050, Spain would reach approximately 200% of its GDP, Portugal and Italy would reach approximately 240% of their GDPs, and the Greek general government consolidated gross debt would exceed 380% of its GDP. Surprisingly, even very optimistic values of GDP growth at 2.5% and real effective interest rates at −0.5% would not be able to bring the debt-to-GDP ratios down noticeably, except for Italy. In addition, the most problematic situation is in Greece, which shows extremely high values, followed by the situation in Spain because GDP growth has a relatively low impact on its debt-to-GDP ratio. Furthermore, the analysis of debt-stabilising primary balances showed that Greece and Italy will not be able to bring their debt-to-GDP ratios to 60% by 2050—provided that no major structural change or government default occurs. Spain and Portugal are in relatively better positions regarding the required sizes of budget balances.

This work analyses the determinants of the EU4 fiscal policies since 1884 to provide a sufficient benchmark for the occurrence between 2000 and 2021.

Arguably, Greece has been more prone to produce deficits when compared to the other EU4 countries. Furthermore, the estimates showed a total inefficiency of the supranational fiscal regulation within the EU and the Euro Area. Arguably, the Euro Area accession motivated the smaller countries to become 'black passengers' by running higher fiscal deficits. The estimates show that the effect of the Euro Area accession was strongly detrimental to Greece. Arguably, the smaller countries (Portugal and Greece) exploited the socialisation of risk in the Euro Area far more than the other two larger countries.

Nevertheless, the two smaller countries were forced to significantly improve their fiscal discipline due to the financial crisis. It should be noted that Greece showed the strongest response to the adverse shock of the COVID-19 crisis, the same as in the case of the previous financial crisis. It is possibly associated with Greece exhibiting higher financial and economic vulnerabilities compared to the other EU4 countries. Nevertheless, the COVID-19 crisis significantly hit all the EU4 countries. Spain showed an even greater fiscal policy reaction to the previous financial crisis.

This work presents estimates of the effects of government expenditure on total output in the EU4 countries—the issue of fiscal policy efficiency. The evidence suggests that the value of the multipliers in the EU4 countries was significantly lower than one before the financial crisis. In particular, 1 euro of government expenditure generated only 0.1–0.8 euros of total output. The fiscal policies of the EU4 countries were highly inefficient and probably crowded out some portion of private investment. One of the possible explanations is the practice of unsustainable and harmful government policies, which systematically stimulated the economies and deepened economic inefficiencies. For instance, the countries' competitiveness and motivation to work were significantly lowered.

Moreover, many job positions and even businesses, which would be unprofitable under normal circumstances, were kept alive. The estimates further suggest that the values of the multipliers in the pre-COVID-19 crisis period were significantly larger, even higher than one, for all the countries except Italy. Nevertheless, the development is not necessarily a sign of more sustainable fiscal and macroeconomic positions of the EU4 countries. The countries had experienced a period of negative output gaps even in the post-recession period. Furthermore, they were arguably less 'overheated' in the subsequent years when compared to the period before the financial crisis. Arguably, it was a temporary phenomenon. It suggests that fiscal austerity without relevant structural reforms is unsuitable for EU4 countries.

Finally, I identified and analysed four main possibilities for dealing with the debts: debt monetisation, fiscal consolidation, structural reforms, and sovereign default. As practised by the ECB, debt monetisation is not an appropriate solution. Its primary effects are based on a short-term perspective, while its secondary effects worsen the situation. Specifically, the effects include higher pressures to the socialisation of risks, moral hazard, and inflationary pressures, often hidden within price bubbles in various asset markets. The crucial aspect is that governments issuing financial instruments experience no relevant feedback that would arise from their expansionary policies. Arguably, the most appropriate solution to the debt crisis is a fiscal consolidation combined with structural reforms that promote long-term economic growth. Unfortunately, the structural reforms must include a return to country-specific currencies in the EU4 countries due to the systemic instabilities in the Euro Area.

Notably, sole fiscal consolidation is not sufficient. In many cases, a return to market principles is needed. It contrasts with the usual short-term reforms focusing on the demand side of the economy. Arguably, the current Euro Area should focus on competitive advantages, long-term policies, and a transparent system design that would not require serious government interventions. Nevertheless, if this option is not politically feasible, a sovereign default will accelerate the functioning of correction mechanisms in the EU and the Euro Area. If the monetary union is not reformed, I do not see a way for these countries to prosper. It will likely result in a further reduction of the living standards. However, it will affect the whole European continent.

MIX
Papier aus verantwortungsvollen Quellen
Paper from responsible sources
FSC® C105338
FSC
www.fsc.org

If you have any concerns about our products,
you can contact us on
ProductSafety@springernature.com

In case Publisher is established outside the EU,
the EU authorized representative is:
Springer Nature Customer Service Center GmbH
Europaplatz 3, 69115 Heidelberg, Germany

Printed by Libri Plureos GmbH
in Hamburg, Germany